Understanding Children's Development in the Early Years

Understanding Children's Development in the Early Years provides an overview of children's personal, social, emotional and moral development, so that practitioners come to understand the complex interaction of factors that give children an individual profile of abilities and differences.

Christine Macintyre has worked with practitioners in many settings and has gathered a range of frequently asked questions from both experienced and new staff. Here, she provides strategies and 'solutions' that practitioners can amend to suit individual children or groups of children in their own learning environments.

- How can I make recording observations meaningful and relevant?
- Are there critical learning times for acquiring different skills?
- How can I help a child cope with bereavement?
- Why do some children bully others?
- Why have some children difficulty in coping in the early years setting?
- What can I do to help children find a friend?

Understanding the answers to these questions will help practitioners establish a positive, caring and friendly learning environment, build relationships between parents, carers and professionals and encourage children to thrive in the nursery setting.

Full of helpful advice for early years practitioners on how to enhance our understanding of very young children, this highly practical book contains many examples taken from a variety of real-life nursery practices and case studies that provide interesting and thought-provoking scenarios.

Books in the *Essential Guides for Early Years Practitioners* series address key issues for early years practitioners working in today's nursery and school environments. Each title is packed full of practical activities, illustrations, support, advice and guidance, all of which is in line with current Government early years policy.

Christine Macintyre was formerly senior lecturer in Child Development, Play and Special Needs at Edinburgh University. She now works as an Early Education Consultant.

The Nursery World/Routledge Essential Guides for Early Years Practitioners

Books in this series address key issues for early years practitioners working in today's nursery and school environments. Each title is packed full of practical activities, support, advice and guidance, all of which is in line with current Government early years policy. The authors use their experience and expertise to write accessibly and informatively, emphasising through the use of case studies the practical aspects of the subject, whilst retaining strong theoretical underpinnings throughout.

These titles will encourage the practitioner and student alike to gain greater confidence and authority in their day-to-day work, offering many illustrative examples of good practice, suggestions for further reading and many invaluable resources. For a handy, clear and inspirational guide to understanding the important and practical issues, the early years practitioner or student need look no further than this series.

Titles in the series:

Circle Time for Young Children
  – Jenny Mosley

Developing Positive Behaviour in the Early Years
  – Sue Roffey

**Identifying Additional Learning Needs in the Early Years:
Listening to the children**
  – Christine Macintyre

Observing, Assessing and Planning for Children in the Early Years
  – Sandra Smidt

Encouraging Creative Play in the Early Years (forthcoming)
  – Diane Rich

Understanding Children's Development in the Early Years

Questions practitioners frequently ask

Christine Macintyre

Routledge
Taylor & Francis Group

LONDON AND NEW YORK

**NURSERY
WORLD**

First published 2007
by Routledge
2 Park Square, Milton Park, Abingdon, Oxon, OX14 4RN

Simultaneously published in the USA and Canada
by Routledge
270 Madison Ave, New York, NY 10016

Routledge is an imprint of the Taylor & Francis Group, an informa business

Typeset in Perpetua by
Florence Production Ltd, Stoodleigh, Devon
Printed and bound in Great Britain by
MPG Books Ltd, Bodmin

British Library Cataloguing in Publication Data
A catalogue record for this book is available from the British Library

Library of Congress Cataloging in Publication Data
Macintyre, Christine, 1938–
    Understanding children's development in the early years:
questions practitioners frequently ask/Christine Macintyre.
        p. cm. – (The Nursery world/Routledge essential guides
    for early years practitioners)
    1. Education, Preschool.   2. Child development.   I. Title.
    II. Series.
    LB1140.2.M325 2007
    305.231 – dc22   2006034789

ISBN10: 0–415–41287–0 (hbk)
ISBN10: 0–415–41288–9 (pbk)
ISBN10: 0–203–96353–9 (ebk)

ISBN13: 978–0–415–41287–2 (hbk)
ISBN13: 978–0–415–41288–9 (pbk)
ISBN13: 978–0–203–96353–1 (ebk)

Contents

Illustrations

FIGURES

TABLES

Acknowledgements

There are many children and early years professionals who have contributed to this book and I should like to thank them all. Both the children and the adults asked fascinating and searching questions that covered the span of children's early development. 'Why do you want to know all this anyway?' asked Ben, aged 4! And when I said goodbye, he queried, 'Have you got all the answers now?'

All the participants have been endlessly patient in sharing their achievements, debating their dilemmas and voicing their concerns. We hoped that the experience of being involved in the research that prompted this text could be useful to other practitioners as they sought to provide the very best education for their own children in their settings and so we set out our findings and the different viewpoints and pieces of advice that came from both experienced and new practitioners.

The text has been illustrated by the children from Early Years (Scotland) Nurseries and from Greenhall Community School in Stafford. Thank you to the parents who gave permission for the photographs to be used and also to the nurseries and school practitioners who provided the learning opportunities that gave such lovely pictures.

Thank you, too, to the staff at Routledge for their patience with me and their expert handling of the text. Having cheerful and helpful responses encourages us to keep thinking and sorting material so that we can say to Ben, 'Well maybe we didn't find all the answers, but we tried hard to discover useful things.' In the end we hope that our readers will understand 'why we wanted to know all of this anyway!' and stay with us on our next voyage of discovery.

Christine Macintyre

Introduction
Setting the scene

It goes without saying that everyone wants their children to be happy at school especially in their first, early years setting. Many, even most children have a wonderful learning experience in a nursery where the three Rs, i.e. Respect, Relationships and Responsive Care (Scottish Executive 2005), guide both planning and practice. In a secure, caring setting, children develop their social, intellectual, emotional, moral and motor skills as they play. They develop a sense of self through recognising their own aptitudes and interests; they learn about other cultures and share new festivals, lifestyle practices and foods. They learn to co-operate with others, to develop empathy with those less fortunate than themselves and, through successfully confronting many experiences and challenges and enjoying support and careful intervention by committed staff, they become confident, stimulated learners, understanding the basis of citizenship.

This is the ideal.

Sadly, however, there are rapidly increasing numbers of children who need additional support if they are to benefit from this very important time. Despite moves to establish a positive, caring and friendly learning environment (e.g. a 'welcome notice' printed in different languages to greet the parents and children each day, along with smiling practitioners) and many initiatives to build relationships between parents, carers and professionals based on trust and respect (e.g. inviting parents into the nursery to tell the children about their festivals and/or to share their skills), there are times when children do not settle and times when they fail to thrive. Both parents and children may have overwhelming personal home issues such as separation, divorce, settling into an alien culture, even not having enough money for food or to pay the rent. There may also be nursery issues, e.g. being bullied, or 'not being able to make a friend' (even though staff do their best to see that this does not happen).

Some children may resent having to follow an unfamiliar routine when they would prefer to be doing something else, even though they may not be able to say what that might be. Although these problems can be difficult to share, once positive relationships have been established, staff and parents can work together to find ways to resolve them.

But there are also 'conflict issues' with parents and/or carers who may have very different notions about the purpose of their child's time in school or their child's 'success' in the nursery setting, even about the friendships their children develop – and these can be hard to solve. As a result, even experienced early years practitioners, head teachers and managers can be left with questions that defy quick or easy answers. These professionals explain that within one group of children,

> We have academically able children who need an extended curriculum; we have children with global developmental delay who need reinforcement and overlearning of the most basic things; some who want to participate in all the activities and some that won't join in at all. We have children with physical difficulties such as cerebral palsy that shouldn't be bumped and one or two children who only know how to barge. We have to support them all. We have to provide challenges for them all and recognise when they succeed. It's a wonderful job, but it's complex and in this culture of litigation, full of risks that we might inadvertently offend. This is a huge concern. Some days, on top of all this and especially when staff are

FIGURE 0.1 Sam is investigating where birds nest

ill or resources get vandalised or even when the weather's really bad and the children can't get outside to play, we are left asking, 'What can we do?'.

Anna, a newly appointed teacher, explains her philosophy:

We try to find a balance between being very open and friendly and supportive to each parent and child and establishing a routine that gives the children security and allows the staff to establish a curriculum that extends their interests and their learning. If we are to monitor the children's progress, we need to plan appropriate activities and organise the resources to allow us to do this. We also want to share our findings with the parents and find if they are happy with how their child is doing or if we should be adjusting our curriculum in any way. Most parents understand how complex this is and they are ready to co-operate and make suggestions and contributions. They give us positive feedback most of the time. But some parents seem to think that nursery is only free childminding so we have to set 'rules' e.g. we tell them, 'Your children do best when they arrive at the correct time, wide awake, ready to enjoy the nursery routine.' Although we understand the extreme difficulties some parents face and we wonder how we would cope, we have to establish ground rules too. We understand 'legitimate reasons' and we can provide breakfast snacks or extra scarves and gloves. None of that is a problem, but frustration builds up when 3-year-olds tell us, 'We were skiving off yesterday. We slept in and then watched the telly.' And they do!

Practitioners just at the start of their careers have many more day-to-day questions about doing their job. Sharon, a first-year nursery nurse student on placement, explains:

I am supposed to be observing a small group of children and looking out over the others but they rush around all the time. I try to find out what they are doing but they won't wait. I just don't know what to write down. I made some notes yesterday saying Max knew his colours and I thought I'd better check it out today. He got them all wrong and rushed off to play in the water. My other notes are just rubbish. What am I going to say at today's staff meeting? I don't seem to have noticed anything useful at all.

I should think that all nursery staff could sympathise with Sharon. She is finding observation is a skill that is acquired slowly, especially when children, as she says, 'won't wait'. Perhaps, as a starter, she could make a chart and ask the more experienced members of staff to give her ideas about specific things to observe. Then, when she gains confidence and greater insight into the particular child being observed, she can take a more open-ended stance and record what she sees, knowing it will be useful. At first recording details can seem a bit tedious, but it is only when a number of observations come together (e.g. in another area Max may have spoken about a *blue truck* or a *red bus* and another member of staff could then confirm that he does know his colours) that assessments can come alive and contribute to a profile of the child's development.

Nursery nurse Jason has been four years in the same setting and has built sound relationships with the families who come to the nursery, yet there are still issues that perplex him and cause him to reflect and ask the question 'why?'. In this instance he explains,

> I have three children from the same family in my nursery. The two boys appear confident and carefree while the little girl, Ali, the youngest one is withdrawn and shy. When she came with Mum and the boys to nursery and went home again, she seemed quite interested in what was going on. But now that she has the chance to stay, she won't. Every day she cries and wants to go home. None of us anticipated this and Mum wants to go back to work. She seems to be blaming us and she tells us that her job can't be interrupted by calls. What can we do?

Ali is probably sensing that Mum needs to get away and she is feeling insecure. She won't know Mum's workplace and so her worries overwhelm the advantages of being familiar with the nursery. It is difficult to anticipate how children will react when asked to spend time apart from their parents; and the fact that her brothers settled easily won't really help, especially if Mum makes comparisons in Ali's hearing. Perhaps there is a quiet corner where she could play with just one or two caring children? Once she can establish a secure space and a friend, she might become more confident. But the main thing is to have patience, and in the meantime to try to distract her – possibly by giving her a special task, e.g. setting out a snack, or making a necklace for her Mum. This can be added to by giving her some gentle, and possibly private, positive feedback.

Connor is a special needs assistant with responsibility for Jay, a 5-year-old with Asperger's syndrome, and also needs to spend some time with the other children. Jay is very bright, but because of Jay's difficulties in interacting with other children, Connor is fascinated to learn how children develop social skills and how poor communication hinders learning. He has found it difficult to enhance the social skills of Tim, a 4-year-old for whom he is also responsible. Tim's parents have not alerted the nursery to any problem. Connor asks,

> How can I get children to make the move from playing alone to playing together? I understand Jay's social difficulties and I am working on helping him to recognise the feelings that come over in facial expressions. But I'm not sure how to support Tim. He is very solitary. He is happy if he is left to play alone, but even when we sit on the carpet for story he moves away from the child beside him, no matter who it is. He reacts angrily, punching and spitting if we try to shift him. It would help him if he could be more relaxed and sociable before he goes to the next class. How can we help him?

Tim is obviously a very unhappy, insecure little boy. Helping him to tolerate other children is not easy and needs infinite patience. Connor could try thinking of ways to gradually reduce the space between Tim and another child, e.g. giving him a beanbag to sit on at story and very gradually moving that nearer a child on a another beanbag might work, because the beanbag might mark 'his space' and help him feel secure. But this will take time.

It might be helpful to find the activity that Tim enjoys best and then find someone with the same interests to share the activity with him. It is the *activity* rather than the person that is important. Tim enjoys building pathways in the sand, but gives up his game when other boys or girls approach. Perhaps he is afraid that tossed sand will get in his eyes. Perhaps, like Jay, he is recognising his social difficulties, for example, not being able to read the non-verbal communication of other children and so not being able to respond appropriately. Allowing him to stay at the sand alone and then with just one other quiet child, e.g. gentle, easy-going Max, is worth a try, especially if he knows the other children are busy with other activities and won't intrude. If that worked, then perhaps Mum could ask that child home, so that building up a friendship is possible. Would Tim allow Max to play nearby? As he has Asperger's, he wouldn't make any social demands yet they each would sense the other was there.

It is also important to find out if Tim's parents find his solitariness an issue at home. Perhaps they are loners too and don't see the need for social interaction. Perhaps they have very different ideas about what is best for Tim.

Of course, suggesting things to parents can be hard, as they may interpret ideas or strategies to help as a criticism of the way they are bringing up their child. It is even trickier if parents' views and nursery views on what is best for the child conflict. Emily, a very experienced nursery teacher, tells of such an issue. She explains:

> Lee is a great child and can happily paint and do craft and bake – he enjoys everything we have to offer. But his Mum wants him to learn to read and write and when she brings him to nursery she always leaves him with 'Go and find a book now . . . or do your writing'. I tried to explain that formally teaching reading and writing isn't really part of our curriculum, that he'll do that at the next stage. But some children, particularly the girls, I find enjoy fine motor skills like writing so we do provide opportunities for emergent writing but we would never force a child because they all develop control at different times.

FIGURE 0.2 Lee and Eli practise emergent writing. Lee doesn't find writing much fun!

FIGURE 0.3 Every day children enjoy stories, learn descriptive words and come to understand the sequence of events

> We have lots of books and we encourage all the children to browse and explain what they see in the pictures and every day they join in storytelling.

Lee's Mum is anxious, as many parents are, because they do not appreciate the vast amount of learning that *precedes* more formal education and how this is all covered in the nursery, play-based curriculum. Perhaps at a parents' evening this could be explained or instances of opportunities for word recognition and emergent writing/number could be pointed out? Some nurseries have a leaflet for parents to study at home, but sometimes this isn't enough. Practitioners have always to remember that some parents might also have difficulties reading English. If parents request more detail, perhaps the nursery could invest in a book to lend, e.g. 'Planning the pre-5 setting' (see Macintyre and McVitty, 2003 for details). Then the parents will be sure that their children are not 'just playing' and this will allow them to recognise the stress-free learning that develops as children play.

Perhaps even more delicate and challenging is knowing what best to say and do when a child experiences bereavement for the first time. Dave was shattered to find he had no words to comfort Rachael, whose grandpa had died. Moreover, he was unsure of the faith status of the little girl or the family and, in the light of the health and safety policy, was unable to offer a hug in place of words. He explains:

> Rachael rushed up to me and said, 'Grandpa's gone.' I didn't know what had happened so I asked, 'Gone where?' The tears welled up so I knew and felt absolutely dreadful. 'I don't know,' Rachael whispered, but then she smiled and added, 'but he'll come back when he's better, won't he?' What could I say?

And what is the best way forward when staff suspect a child may have an additional learning need, and parents deny that this is the case? This happened to Maria. She explains:

> We have this little boy Omar, who is 14 months. He is very floppy and makes no attempt to pull himself up to standing even when he is wanting out of his cot. He is sitting unsupported for very brief spells but soon topples over. His Mum says she has taken him to their GP and has been told there is nothing wrong. In the nursery we are unsure whether there is something really wrong or whether he will get stronger as he matures. He is always first into nursery at 8 a.m. and last to be picked up at 6 in the evening. What happens in between we don't know, but we suspect he's put to bed with not much stimulation? What should we do?

These cases are tricky. The parents have to agree to contact being made with the health visitor, who would be the key person for a child of this age. The cut-off point between delayed development (where hopefully the child will catch up once he matures and gets stronger) and the signs of a syndrome (such as dyspraxia, for example, where early intervention is essential) is not clearly defined. If the parents do not wish the nursery to contact the health visitor and concerns continue, then building up a friendly relationship with the parent(s) is the best way. Giving positive feedback (e.g. 'Omar stretched out and held his car for quite a time and chortled with happiness today') may help them relax and see that you would like to build a partnership to support their child. They may be very unhappy about the child's progress but could be at the stage of denying that anything is amiss. Pointing out positive things is a subtle way of indicating the level of what is being achieved – but this strategy needs time, patience and tact. On the other hand, Omar's Mum might feel inadequate and believe that the nursery environment is better then the one she can provide at home. Eventually, if staff consider that the child is being harmed by non-action, then the nursery or school head teacher would decide the next steps. No nursery practitioner should act alone.

All of these and many more questions that practitioners have asked will permeate the text of this book. The answer often suggested in the literature is 'get to know each individual child and show him you respect his ideas and his background' – and indeed this is an admirable ambition. However, success also depends on understanding the different aspects of development and how they interact in often very different environments to produce children who can give such pleasure and such anguish, who are full of surprises and who never fail to let adults know that they are there.

The purpose of this book is to explain how these different aspects of development interact and to consider the range of influences that make children who they are. It will also tackle difficult questions that various practitioners have raised, hoping that the answers will allow other practitioners to adapt the suggested strategies to suit their own children in their particular environment – even if the solutions raise more complex issues as they unfold.

Chapter 1

Observing children's development in the nursery

Q Why is understanding development and observation the cornerstone of education in the early years?

Because education in the early years settings is child-centred. This means that the staff observe the children carefully, and monitor and record what they do in each aspect of their development – social, emotional, intellectual, moral and motor. The information is recorded, dated and discussed so that a full and accurate profile of each child's progress is built up over time. The observations also pinpoint what teaching input each child requires and so can be used in planning the programme of opportunities and experiences that will promote each child's learning. They also identify particular strengths so that staff can prepare extension work. This may be in the form of resources, e.g. a book that matches the child's interests or craft materials that enable the child to complete a piece of work to a high level. Observations can also highlight any difficulties that need special intervention, e.g. if a child was finding it difficult to cross the midline of the body, then the ability to crawl would be checked, for this competence is needed to develop cross-lateral co-ordination. It is very important that individual gifts and talents across the developmental spectrum are fostered, and that needs are identified, monitored and, hopefully, alleviated, possibly even before the child knows they are there.

Q So observations and recordings are used to plan the day? This doesn't sound too taxing – why do people say it's difficult?

It takes time to master the skill of observing children, i.e. to develop eyes that can spot individual differences. This is because there is just so much to see and rarely will the children sit and wait while practitioners check their recordings. They are usually anxious to get on with the business of playing, not really aware that observers might be left behind. This is why practitioners often feel overwhelmed by recording examples of behaviour that can build into a useful profile of a child's progress. However, when they see how different recordings (always named and dated) come together, they can be convinced that their own detail is valuable in compiling a meaningful picture. Sometimes, experienced and new observers may see different things when they observe the same child, but this can add to the richness of discussion. Having the observer's name added to the recording can also show the range of things each observer sees. The best plan is to video the children, especially when these discrepancies occur, for then the tape can be replayed and paused at relevant points, giving observers time to review their observations, possibly from a different perspective. Having a video also lets absent staff or parents share specially interesting moments of progress.

Q But what should we look for? Do we just note anything that we think would be of interest?

KEY TOPIC

Observing and recording

Sometimes staff can be asked to observe a specific competence, e.g. 'Time on task' as a means of gathering evidence to ascertain a child's attention span, or whether the children were limiting learning by being too attached to one area or one toy. In that case staff might be asked: 'Record how long Sharon stays at each activity and note what she chooses to do.' This time-sampling method would limit what was to be noted. This observation is not asking for quality, i.e. how well Sharon does or what language she uses when she interacts with other children. Only a time-frame is required. Noting the purpose of the observation is useful as a reference for later reflection on progress (see Table 1.1, overleaf).

This observation, combined with a number of others, confirms the practitioner's fears that Sharon's behaviour is bordering on being obsessive, so the staff discuss what to do. Should they hide the pram? Would this force Sharon to choose something else or would it take away her security? Should they ignore the behaviour hoping that other interests will take over as Sharon becomes more confident in the nursery? Answers to questions like this depend on knowing the child well and anticipating her reactions. This is what makes planning based on observations so time-consuming and difficult, but so vitally important.

▉ TABLE 1.1 Time sampling (1)

Planned time: every 3 minutes	*Child*: Sharon. *Observer*: Leanne Observation to find time spent on one activity. Query obsession.
13.00	Searches for pram, grabs the handle and wanders round the outside of the room. She doesn't check if the doll is inside. She is rocking the pram fiercely and watching the wheels spin.
13.03	Sally asks for the pram. Sharon glares and tries to push the pram into her – Sally retreats, putting out her tongue.
13.06	Jackie approaches and they go to the house area together, Sharon is still gripping the pram. She struggles to get it inside, ignoring pleas to 'Leave it at the door'.
13.09	They settle there. Sharon tries to close the door.
13.12	They have made a tea party. She still holds the pram.
13.15	Jackie asks if the doll wants tea. Sharon shakes her head. She has never looked for the doll. The pram is the important thing.
13.20	Jackie has fetched a different doll. The tea party resumes.

A second example concerns Sean. Staff are gathering evidence to show how his aggressive behaviour is affecting his social skills (see Table 1.2).

▉ TABLE 1.2 Time sampling (2)

Name:	Sean aged 4.8 (second year in nursery). Observation: no. 8 this term
Time	**Observed activity**
9.00	Races into room, throws coat into corner and won't say 'Good morning'.
9.01	Turns and hits another boy, then heads for the large construction area where he dismantles a 'castle', knocking the bricks roughly to the floor.
9. 05	Sits beside the teacher facing the group to sing 'Good Morning to everyone' jingle. Scowls when asked to join the others.
9.07	Can't relax – shoulders very tense. Asks: 'When can I get the bricks?'
9.08	Teacher asks him to sit quietly for a moment more. He struggles up and runs across the room. He bangs into a table and yells out about his sore leg.
9.10	He has found his coat and yells out, 'I'll tell my mother on you.'

TABLE 1.3 Example of three-day observation

Name: Janna   Date: 14.10.06–17.10.06

Observer: Helen	Yes, can do	No, cannot do
Can crawl		*
Can stand and sit still	*	
Can pick up small objects using the pincer grip		*
Can hold a paintbrush comfortably	*	
Can climb on the frame		*
Can cope independently at the toilet		*
Can balance on a wide bench	*	
Can control a pencil		*

A ten-minute observation like this details reactions and attitudes. It provides evidence of Sean's anxiety and would be collated with other recordings so that an emotional profile could be produced for a psychologist should there be need for expert support.

Another observation might concern movement skills. In this case, the competences to be observed are set out and there is a three-day time scale (see Table 1.3 above).

However, there are times when staff are given one child or a small group to observe and they are asked to 'record what you see', often on sticky labels that can later be put together in a file. These then form the basis of discussions with more and less experienced practitioners all making contributions.

28.11.06

Martin is confident on the climbing frame. He can explain what he wants to do and knows 'I can jump higher than anyone else in the nursery.'

Aim: To set out a difficult challenge with ropes and hurdles and see if he can negotiate that and self-evaluate his performance.

FIGURE 1.1 Sticky label recording

Q Our curriculum is all about play. What contribution does play make to social development in the pre-school years?

Susan Isaacs (1933) has produced a lovely response. She explained,

Play is a child's life and the means by which he comes to understand the world about him.

She identified and showed the value of play all those years ago, and in a developmental way described the different stages of understanding. The first stage was the children learning to gain attention and building a relationship with family and carers; then they progressed to identifying the properties of objects; and later still the modes of behaviour appropriate in different environments. Then, children who can move around set themselves problem-solving opportunities, e.g. 'how do I empty this cupboard?'. Unfortunately, this never seemed to lead to 'and how do I put the things back?'.

■ FIGURE 1.2
Amy is learning to co-ordinate two hands doing different things at the midline of the body

She is learning about the consistency of clay and how to mould it. She may continue to make something or, if the clay falls apart, she may abandon what she is doing; but she will still have developed both intellectual and motor skills.

During play, the children have the opportunity to experiment and develop their creativity without fear of failing to meet some pre-set standard and without having to complete anything if that is their wish. They learn from watching others in their peer group who are likely to be playing at a similar developmental level and therefore doing things that should be within their grasp too. So they learn from absorbing ideas that extend their own thinking rather than waiting for intervention from an adult.

Q Can practitioners observe children's difficulties as they play?

Skilled observers can identify children who show their anxieties at play. Children who smack dolls excessively might be acting out abuse they experience at home, although, strangely, many children who have never been smacked appear to think this is the way to behave. Practitioners have to be sure of their ground before alerting health visitors or social services, but at the same time they should not delay too long. Again, dated and detailed recordings are essential. If this can be supported by video, then this provides the clearest picture.

The earliest indications of additional learning needs can also be identified. First, let's think about speech and language difficulties. Hopefully, children will be relaxed as they play and may be able to speak with greater fluency than in a more formal situation. Moreover, they should be being stimulated by something that interests them. If they still can't talk, observers must find out if, despite not talking, they understand the development of the play. This assessment differentiates between delay and impairment. Parents can also let the practitioners know if the children speak at home, for some children may choose not to speak in strange surroundings (elective mutism). But usually in play children learn reciprocity, turn-taking and new words. If they find communicating with their peers difficult, if other children can't understand what they say, then specialist help from a speech and language therapist should be sought.

Poor muscle tone in the big muscle groups that control gross movements can be observed most easily when children play outdoors, for poor balance and control will cause them to stumble and fall. Children with poor co-ordination will often avoid activities that would help them develop the very skills they require, e.g. learning to ride a bike. So it is a good idea for bikes and trikes with different levels of demand to be

FIGURE 1.3 Helena is developing her sense of balance in a safe yet challenging activity

available so that every child can have a chance of gaining the confidence to ride.

Indoors, if the children have difficulty controlling a pencil or threading beads, then this can also indicate dyspraxia. Poor movement ability could be symptomtic of many very different difficulties, however, so quick assessments should not be made and labels should not be applied without careful testing by a psychologist.

Then there are the children who avoid nursery rhymes and other rhythmical activities. This can be an sign of dyslexia and early intervention with clapping games can help. Practitioners should also involve the children in 'listening to sounds' games, because poor sound differentiation can also be a sign of dyslexia.

So play provides wonderful learning experiences for the children and diagnostic opportunities for the staff. Whether difficulties will be resolved by maturation is a taxing question. If, however, any difficulty significantly affects the child's competence over a period of three weeks or so, then a more formal diagnosis of a specific difficulty may need to be made by the appropriate agency, e.g. a speech and language therapist.

Q But why should making observations like this be so difficult?

The complexity comes from the fact that each child is an individual, an active learner in a social setting, and what each child brings to that setting and how each child responds to the people and the activities there depends on a large number of developmental and environmental factors. Different children also learn in different ways, so they are usually interested in activities that reflect their preferences, i.e. either listening to instructions or stories if they are strong auditory learners (the listeners); looking and gleaning information from things they see if they are visual learners (the lookers); and touching, feeling and moving if they relate best to kinaesthetic cues (the doers) (see Chapter 2 for more information).

Another challenge for staff observing young children is that the rate they progress doesn't follow a simple curve. Sometimes children are slow to grasp ideas but, once they do, they bound ahead. Others grasp the ideas quickly, but after some initial rapid progress, they can appear to stick for a while; then something clicks (possibly due to a clear explanation, but it could also be that the child will have been mulling ideas over and considering alternatives), and they make progress again.

Q I see. But how are we supposed to cope with all these differences?

One suggestion to make the task more manageable is to divide development into separate aspects or component parts. While this highlights the importance of each aspect, however, practitioners also have to remember that all of the parts interact all of the time, and that this analysis, i.e. considering one at a time, is best seen as a first step before blending the observations back together again to give a full picture.

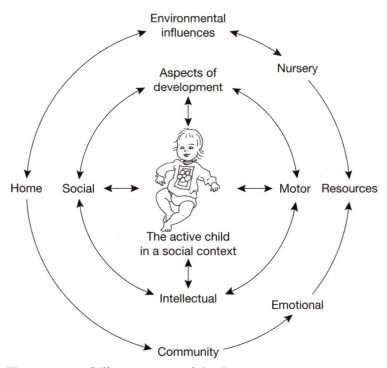

FIGURE 1.4 Different aspects of development

Q Can you give some examples of how the different aspects interact?

Example 1 Let's think about Liam, aged 9 months, who has just learned to crawl. He has mastered a very important skill. This is because crawling involves cross-lateral co-ordination. Establishing this pattern is import-ant for later skills such as writing and other life skills that involve crossing the midline of the body with two hands doing different things at the same time, e.g. zipping up a coat, using a knife and fork, cleaning teeth. In crawling, he is also learning to balance in a safe position and learning about directions and distances as he moves each hand and foot forward. This progress would be recorded under *physical and motor* development.

But acquiring this skill also means that Liam can move around independently and go where he wants to go. This develops his independence and, provided he has no nasty bumps, his confidence grows too. Even with a bump, most children's desire to move around will help them overcome their first frights. They learn they can survive and are intrinsically motivated to keep moving. Their movement has fostered their *emotional* development.

This new skill is bound to involve other people. They will admire Liam's prowess or interact with him in a positive way, even when they are just trying to catch him. Moreover, at playgroup or at home he is now able to join in a game. Even if he is simply chasing after siblings or peers, he is part of a group. His *social* development is enhanced.

And, as crawling allows him to travel further, to solve problems (e.g. how can I get under that stair gate?), even to take risks, he learns about safety (e.g. whether he really can crawl up stairs – the crawling pattern and the climbing one are the same – or what will happen if he tries to pull himself up on an unsteady table). So his *intellectual* development benefits too.

Example 2   For a second example, let's follow 4-year-old Roisin as she threads beads for a necklace for her Mum who has been ill.

Roisin first makes a selection of beads to make a pattern: this involves choosing the colours and the sizes of the beads. This is helping her *intellectual* development. If she chooses to graduate the beads and/or estimates the length of the thread needed to go round Mum's neck, some early mathematical development is happening as well.

Perhaps she may be considering what colours her Mum would prefer to make her feel better – this is the development of empathy (i.e. understanding how another person is feeling) and altruism (i.e. doing a task to give someone else pleasure). These are *emotional* gains.

When the gift has been received, she can be sure of some praise from Mum; and if the necklace is shown around to friends and family, then *socially* she is benefiting from being the centre of attention and learning to receive praise – something some children can find off-putting and strange.

And how is *physical and motor* development enhanced in this activity? Well, to thread the beads, Roisin is practising the pincer grip through using her finger and thumb together to manipulate an object. She is developing control at the midline of the body as she holds the thread poised to penetrate the beads. This skill is also important for controlling a pencil, or paintbrush, or a knife and fork. Finally, a real sense of achievement – watch how her face lights up – enables her to release

19

endomorphins into her bloodstream, promoting the feel-good factor that stimulates us all to try again, and do even more demanding tasks.

But, of course, children don't develop these skills overnight, and some take much longer than others to acquire them at all. These individual differences are what make the study of children's development so fascinating and worthwhile. So, although observations may primarily be focusing on just one aspect of development, progress in one affects all of the others too.

Q Most nurseries arrange their activities by areas such as the 'Home corner' and the 'Water tray' or the 'Art and craft area'. Does each activity area promote all the aspects of development equally well, or, if a child's difficulty is mainly social, will one area offer more support than the others?

That's a very good question and there are two parts to the answer. First, staff have to analyse the potential in each area so that they know and understand the possibilities, then they may have to alter the resources provided in order to promote the kind of learning *required*. Some subtle input can help. Think about baking, and how the children love to mix the margarine and sugar. If there are children with poor strength in their fingers, they should be 'the first mixers' when the margarine is stiff. That means they are having a strengthening session, but the staff will have to plan this by analysing the potential that exists within each activity.

By reading through the material presented in Figure 1.8, it becomes apparent that the children's own inbuilt rate of learning, their preferences and their environment all have a major role to play in enhancing their development. Some children will be inquisitive and use every opportunity to practise skills and learn new things, while others are content to repeat favourite activities and 'stay safe', with no intention of taking risks or pushing back the boundaries of learning at all. Questions about intervening in children's play arise from this. But who knows what the children are imagining as they appear to waste time? Intervention must be carefully planned on the basis of continual observation and in the knowledge of the individual child. A good maxim is: 'When in doubt, keep back. Wait, listen and observe some more!'

Some children can build on opportunities they have already encountered, e.g. dance classes, while others may have visited playgrounds and used their imaginations to 'fly to the sky' on the swings or developed their interest in 'minibeasts' by searching under hedges. Some children

	Home area	Art and craft area	Large construction area	Sand and water trays	Music and dance
Social	• Planning a meal together • Sharing ideas • Waiting to be served	• Discussing ideas for a collage • Sharing resources	• Building together • Sharing ideas and plans	• Planning a road-building scheme – or a water feature with siphons and tubes	• Planning an accompanied dance • Sharing percussion
Intellectual	• 1–1 correspondence in setting tables • Colour matching • Language development	• Learning about mixing colours • Use of different materials and textures	• Organising blocks in height/weight order • Appreciating weights and sizes e.g. 'What will fit?'	• Understanding floating and sinking • Vocabulary extension • Understanding properties of wet and dry sand • Measuring and counting	• Investigating different sounds and how they stimulate different qualities of movement
Emotional	• Role-play – being Dad, Mum, caring for baby	• Appreciating patterns and shapes	• Dealing with frustration when blocks collapse • Pride in completing a construction	• Appreciation of the different elements coming together, e.g. building a fort and a moat	• Appreciating sounds and actions • Enjoying the activities
Moral	• Complying with others' wishes • Making judgements regarding what is right and what is wrong	• Satisfaction in making a gift for someone; or in completing a piece of work	• Looking out for each other when using heavy blocks • Sharing spaces	• Recognising the talents of other children • Considering their wishes and adapting to them	• Identifying preferences • Complying with ideas • Using musical instruments sensitively
Motor	• Handling dishes • Dialling the telephone	• Fine motor control of the brush • Accurate threading • Hand–eye co-ordination	• Lifting and lowering with control • Developing strength and 'finesse' in placing the blocks	• Two hands working together at the midline of the body • Scooping, moulding, firming the sand • Lifting siphons • Control in pouring the water	• Co-ordinating sounds and actions • Balance and control of the body • Developing body and spatial awareness

FIGURE 1.5
Iain is developing his understanding of how snails move; later he will search for a book on 'minibeasts'

will have visited a prison and be able to relate what happens there. Some will be given too much food, while others will not have enough to eat. This is why getting to know each child's background in terms of opportunities and experiences is so important, for children from different home environments will already have different skills and understandings, which will form the basis of further learning. Moreover, the children will expect the practitioners to know all these things without realising that they don't. But when practitioners do discover more about each child's nature, i.e. what children bring into the world, and the effect of nurture, i.e. how they are affected by the environment in which they grow, then the practitioners can develop the individual profile of each child. This can then be used to find the best way to proceed.

Chapter 2

Understanding the earliest development and its impact on learning

Q When does development begin and what sorts of things determine whether children will learn with ease or have difficulties?

Let's go back to the start. At the moment of conception the sperm has travelled up the fallopian tube and pierced the shell of the egg to form the zygote. The combination of genes from the father and from the mother provide a unique genetic pattern and, from that moment in time, and provided there are no accidents during the time of cell division or negative

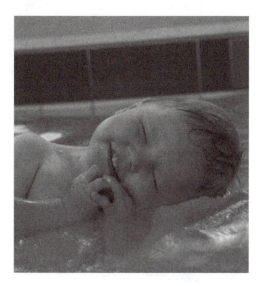

FIGURE 2.1
'Heaven lies about us in our infancy . . .'

Wordsworth, 'Ode on Intimations of Immortality'

influences passed through the placenta (e.g. German measles in the mother affecting hearing and vision in the child), then the 'nature' side of development is set. Already certain characteristics are in place, for example eye colour, body-build and temperament (e.g. whether the child will be outgoing or shy). Some of these attributes can be changed by experiences, e.g. the vulnerable child can learn to be more confident, but new learning or moments of stress can cause the inherited traits to emerge once more. Some features are not amenable to change, e.g. the child who wants to be a jockey but grows to six feet, just has to accept the body-build that was inherited. Growth patterns can only be minimally affected by diet, whereas the weight factor can vary a great deal depending on the quantity and quality of nutrition children have.

Unfortunately, the genetic pattern – 'a genetic blueprint which influences what we can do' (Bee 2002) – may contain difficulties/syndromes such as dyslexia, dyspraxia, autism or some of the more debilitating illnesses such as haemophilia. And, after conception, accidents in cell division can happen which can cause Down's syndrome or even conjoined twins. So, even before we are born, to some extent the die is cast.

Q What happens before we are born? How can that process affect how we learn?

Some time during the first 24 to 36 hours after conception, cell division begins and tendrils are formed which implant these divided cells into the uterine wall. This is the start of the embryonic stage. As the placenta (the connecting tissue that takes oxygen and nutrients to the baby from the mother and removes waste products too) and other support structures are formed, the embryo is separating itself into specialist groups of cells for hair and skin, sensory receptors, muscles, nerve cells and circulatory systems. By the eighth week the embryo is one-and-a-half inches long and has a heart and a basic circulatory system; and by 12 weeks the sex can be determined, eyelids and lips are there, and feet have toes and hands have fingers. For the rest of the period of gestation, the development of the systems continues. The nervous system is one of the least well-developed systems at birth, but maturation is clearly at work. The baby doesn't consciously learn to do certain things; there is an inbuilt pattern of changes that are the same for all children in every culture.

It is fascinating to realise that, even in the womb, babies are developing a whole series of primitive reflexes that will be important for survival at birth and during the first few weeks of life. They are controlled by the brain stem, a vital area that controls breathing and the heartbeat. If these reflexes remain active beyond 6–12 months, however, then that shows a structural weakness within the central nervous system.

One of the reflexes that impacts on children's attitudes and ability to learn is the Moro reflex. It becomes active at 9 weeks *in utero*; it is fully present at birth but should be inhibited, i.e. washed away, by 2–4 months so that more sophisticated reflexes can emerge. The Moro reflex triggers an involuntary reaction to any 'threat', e.g. a sudden loud noise, bright light or sudden movement. It consists of an outward lift of both arms out from the body and the head is thrown back. There is a sudden intake of breath, a rise in blood pressure and the face reddens, showing a release of adrenaline and cortisol into the system. This is a 'fight or flight' response that keeps the baby safe. But if this persists, the children will be in a constant state of alert. They are stressed and tense, waiting for something horrible to occur. They may respond by being aggressive or run from the scene. They are constantly on edge and prone to allergies.

Q How could we observe this in the nursery?

In the nursery, children with a retained Moro reflex will find it hard to settle and listen calmly to stories, or even instructions about activities, apprehensive that some sudden change will occur. They may be hyper-sensitive to noises and, as many books and games have noises as part of their make-up, these may be avoided too. Some children are unable to cut out noises in the environment and will cover their ears. The normal busyness of the day upsets them. The colours of the plastic toys, the smell of soap or chemicals in the toilets, flickering strip lights or humming radiators, even seams in socks, can all be sources of disquiet for the Moro-retentive child.

Q What else develops before birth that has such an influence on how children behave?

Babies also develop spatial awareness in the womb. When they kick, they are developing their kinaesthetic sense, which helps them to judge distances and directions. This kicking action is retained after birth. Then it can be seen as a swimming stroke, for all new babies can swim. Unfortunately, they lose this reflex action and the skill has to be re-learned.

25

Newborns also have a primitive stepping action that is lost in the first two weeks of life.

Before birth, too, the vestibular sense (the sense of balance) helps the baby to get into the correct head-down position to be born. The baby is building a relationship with gravity that will enable him to develop sound movement patterns that can be adapted to different environments as he grows.

AFTER BIRTH: FIRST ASSESSMENTS

The newborn has special tests immediately and then again five minutes later to detect any problems. There are set criteria and the five aspects are monitored to give a composite score of between 0 and 10.

The Apgar Test

See Table 2.1.

Q Do most babies score 10? And if the baby has a low score does this always mean long-lasting concerns or learning difficulties?

Scoring 10 immediately after birth is rare, but at the five-minute test, 85–90 per cent of infants score 9 or 10. A birth score of 7+ indicates there is no danger, while lower scores show that the baby requires help

TABLE 2.1 The Apgar Test

Aspect observed	Score 0	Score 1	Score 10
Heart rate	Absent	< 100 mins	100 mins
Respiratory rate	Not breathing	Weak cry, shallow breathing	Good strong cry and regular breathing
Muscle tone	Flaccid	Some flexion of arms and legs	Well flexed
Response to stimulation of feet	None	Some movement	Cry
Colour	Blue: pale	Body pink, extremities blue	Completely pink

in establishing the normal breathing pattern. Very low-scored babies can survive if they are given appropriate succour and support. This depends on what caused the deficit. A brief lack of oxygen can be overcome, but a neurological deficit may take longer or endure over the lifespan.

THE IMPORTANCE OF NURTURE

Q Surely nurture can only affect the baby after birth?

In the womb, the foetus can be affected by the quality of what travels through the placenta, i.e. the cord that joins the baby to the mother. In the past it was thought that the foetus was totally protected, but newer findings reveal that alcoholism, smoking and illnesses such as Aids can affect the unborn child. So it could be said that nurture is important from conception too.

Q What are the most important factors affecting development and learning in the environment?

The experiences and opportunities the child encounters. (See Chapter 3 for further information about first relationships.)

At birth, the child already has 100,000 million brain cells, which means the brain is already three-quarters the weight of an adult brain. What is different is that vital connections between the cells have not yet been made. While this limits what the baby can do, it also provides flexibility so that connections develop as a result of the baby's experiences. This is the first relationship between nature, i.e. what children are born with, and nurture, i.e. what they come to know as a result of interactions with their family, their environment, and their cultural traditions. It is important to understand the interaction of both nature and nurture, because only then will the way babies change over time be fully understood.

Understanding the nature/nurture debate is important for organising the best kind of education. If the children's environment makes a difference, then early intervention programmes should compensate for less-advantaged homes where resources and/or support may be limited. While some early intervention programmes, e.g. fostering literacy, help disadvantaged children begin their more formal education on a level with their peers, follow-up evaluations found that the initial gains were sometimes lost. This was hugely disappointing. Was it possible that children could learn by rote without having the skills to retain their new understandings or apply them in new contexts? Or perhaps their home environment was so different that the new learning was not important there? Or perhaps the intervention assumed one kind of difficulty and did not meet the range of problems that were present?

Q You said temperament was inherited and could be modified by environmental factors. How can the temperament of young children affect the way they learn?

Some babies seem to be born with calm and sunny natures, while others are fractious and irritable. The fact that two such temperaments can exist in the same family indicate that temperament is innate, i.e. is dependent on 'nature' rather than nurture or environmental influences (e.g. parenting skills, or the quality of diet, or provision of resources). The interesting thing is how a baby's temperament – shown through their responses to overtures – influences their carer, either to keep communicating through smiling and cooing, or to give up and withdraw, possibly because of feeling inadequate for not making the baby smile. So the inborn bias to behave in a certain way has long lasting social/intellectual consequences. And as interactions build up over time, the shy, introverted baby becomes the oversensitive or withdrawn child.

'Resilience' and 'vulnerability' are another set of constructs. In the same situation, resilient children will focus on the positive elements and be ready to try again, while the vulnerable ones will dwell on the negative points and become downhearted and sad. It is not difficult to imagine the devastating effect of teasing or bullying on vulnerable children, who find it impossible to laugh off hurtful remarks. And even if these don't occur, vulnerable children anticipate that they may. They respond by becoming isolated; or they use other inappropriate ways of behaving, and end up being blamed.

Yet another set of temperamental characteristics are 'impulsiveness and reflectiveness'. The impulsive child acts immediately without regard for the consequences, while the reflective child, pondering on all the possibilities, may not get round to acting at all. The impulsive child will finish early, with many slips, because he does not listen to instructions properly, while the reflective child finds too many confusing possibilities and so finishes late, if at all.

In general, environmental influences are not strong enough to overcome the effects of innate characteristics. Children with the attention disorders ADD (attention deficit disorder) and ADHD (attention deficit hyperactivity disorder) show extreme examples of this, although it has to be remembered that these disorders have a neurological basis – they are not just restless children uninterested in what they have to do.

Although some polar examples have been given here, it must be remembered that these characteristics are on a continuum, with no exact cut-off points to differentiate between those who have one characteristic or another. Children described as introverted can become more confident when support is given, but without repeated reinforcement, they tend to lack self-belief in their own abilities. And even when they are successful, they may well be waiting for this to disappear, and they fall back on their inbuilt insecurity. The important point is that these inherited traits are relatively stable, especially in new situations, and they influence how children respond to tasks, to offers of friendship, to the chance to take risks. In the same situation a pessimistic child sees a 'gift box' as half empty, while the optimist sees it as nearly full or if not, immediately makes plans to fill it.

DOMINANT AND RECESSIVE GENES

Q So, if the mother and father are the same and the pattern of maturation is the same, why are children in the same family, who have largely the same experiences, as different as 'chalk and cheese'? Is it because they have inherited different genes?

The combination of genes from the father in the sperm and the mother in the ovum creates a unique genotype. The nucleus of each cell in the body (except the sperm and the ovum) contains 46 chromosomes arranged in 23 pairs. The sperm and the ovum have 23 chromosomes, instead of 23 pairs, and at conception they combine to form the 23 pairs.

Because the baby inherits two chromosomes – one from each parent – the genetic instructions may be the same (homozygous) or different (heterozygous). Children born to one tall and one short parent most often measure somewhere in between the two – in this case the two developmental signals appear to blend. More unusually, e.g. with blood type, a child can have both characteristics: the child who receives an A-type from one parent and a B-type from the other may have an AB-type. More usually, though, one gene is dominant and one recessive. The dominant gene 'wins' for this generation and will be the only characteristic expressed. But the non-dominant or recessive gene can stay as part of the genotype and be passed on to the next generation. This is why parents, observing their children, often say, 'Isn't that Grandma or Grandpa all over again?'.

A number of inherited diseases such as cystic fibrosis or disabilities, e.g. autism, appear to be passed on through the function of dominant and recessive genes. If a recessive gene is involved, it must come from both parents. A carrier is someone who inherits the disease from one parent: this person will not have the disease but may pass it on to the next generation, and in some cases the disease can become more severe.

Sometimes parents, anxious to know what has caused their child's disability, are asked to reflect on the illness or the behaviour pattern of the previous generation. Only then do they realise that strange but minor eccentricities in grandparents may be multiplied to revel themselves as disabilities in their children. Charlotte Moore (2004), who has two autistic sons, recounts how, when the family reflected, they remembered an uncle who collected dust in jars. Still, this one trait had not caused the family to consider him autistic. Research is still trying to unlock the secrets of this complex code.

Twins and siblings

A multiple birth has a probability of one in a hundred, with the great majority being twin births. About two-thirds of twins are fraternal twins, where more than one ovum has been produced, that is, each has been fertilised by a separate sperm. These twins are not alike genetically and may well be made up of one boy and one girl. The remaining one-third are identical twins developing from the same single fertilised ovum, which, during the process of cell division, has split, with each part developing into a separate individual. These babies have identical genetic heritages. Late cell division may cause 'mirror' twins, where each is a mirror image of the other (one right-handed, one left-handed) or, in the saddest of cases, conjoined twins.

GENDER DIFFERENCES

Q Why are there differences in the development of boys and girls?

Girls show slightly faster pre-natal development, i.e. they are one to two weeks ahead in skeletal development at birth. So, even though boys tend to be longer and heavier, the girls have greater bone strength.

Pre-birth, boys are more vulnerable than girls and feature more in spontaneous abortions. This vulnerability continues through the lifespan, as can be seen in the shorter predicted lifespan for males. Boys also feature much more frequently in the numbers needing additional support. The boy:girl ratio is high in dyspraxia, 5:1; dyslexia, 5:1; ADHD, 5:1; and so on. Questions as to why this should be abound, with no definitive answers yet.

Although boys are often taller than girls, this may not be so in the primary school years. Adolescence occurs earlier for girls and their growth spurt happening around age 12 can leave the boys far behind in terms of height. But then the boys shoot up and overtake the girls in both height and strength.

Q Do big children do better that little ones? Why should this be?

Certainly not always. But there is evidence that parents and teachers have higher expectations of big children, tending to judge them by their size rather than their chronological age. They are given more responsibility and often rise to the challenge.

GROWTH AND MATURATION

Q What's the difference between *growth* and *maturation*?

Growth is the pattern of physical changes that are laid down at conception. In the baby physical development is cephalocaudal, i.e. head to toe and proximo-distal, i.e. from centre to periphery. That is why babies hold up their heads before they sit, and sit before they pull up to stand. These patterns are universal, i.e. they happen for all children in the same way. Physical growth is much slower between the ages of 2 and 6 than in the earlier period. Between age 2 and adolescence, children grow in height by 2 to 3 inches per year.

Maturation is often described as a biological clock. Maturation is responsible for the infant who changes from crawling to walking because he has the neurological connections and musculature to let it happen. It controls hormone input at adolescence and the skin losing elasticity in old age. We are powerless to control this; we can neither hurry it up nor slow it down.

31

And each change brings psychological links (confidence and independence) that enable cognition to broaden the horizons, undertake a greater range of experiences and learn more. If both genetic gifts and environmental inputs are favourable, the children will be fortunate indeed.

KEY TOPIC

Understanding sensory perception and integration

Q **When I tell the children about their senses, I talk about seeing and hearing and touching and smelling and tasting – the five senses. But hearing about the kinaesthetic makes me ask, are there more?**

Yes, there are eight. Let's make a list and then have an explanation because all the senses work together to help children to move around and to learn. It's important when thinking about sensitivity, to understand 'hyper' (over) and 'hypo' (under), because these indicate the level of awareness present. Dr Robert Winston (2006) in the series 'Child of Our Time' is investigating synaesthesia. He claims that babies' senses are much more colourful and used 'less separately' than ours. Adults with different degrees of synaesthesia may dream in colour or in another language, even one they claim they do not know. They may find that one sense conjures up unbidden images, e.g. the sight of a piece of cake at teatime allowed Marcel Proust to smell the perfume of the flowers in his aunt's garden, and remember all the vibrant colours and the scents that were part of his childhood. So we should not be dismissive of children's 'stories' that seem to us to be rather far-fetched. They may be using all of their senses together and giving us the benefit of their sensitive perception.

THE SENSES

See Table 2.2 for a summary of the senses.

The vestibular sense

The first of the senses to be developed before birth is the vestibular sense, or sense of balance. It is situated in the inner ear with the auditory or hearing sense and is the leader of the sensory orchestra because all sensations must pass through the vestibular sense en route to the cerebral cortex, the thinking part of the brain. In the womb, the vestibular sense gets the baby the right way up to be born. Breech babies may have a poor sense of balance (because the vestibular sense was weak before birth) and a poor sense of hand dominance. After the birth, the vestibular sense

TABLE 2.2 The senses

The senses	Their key role	Indicators of difficulties
Vestibular	Balance	Unsteadiness; unwilling to leave the ground or take risks, e.g. using a tricycle or climbing frame
Kinaesthetic	Spatial awareness	Unable to judge distances; bumping and spilling; knocking things over
Proprioceptive	Body awareness	General clumsiness; not knowing where the body parts are
Visual	Seeing and tracking (functional sight)	Squinting; rubbing eyes; holding a book too near or far from the face
Auditory	Listening and hearing	Distractibility; inability to focus
Tactile	Feeling and touching	Needs firm touch or can't bear to be touched; 'hyper' or 'hypo' reaction to pain and temperature
Taste and smell	Accept /reject food Judge distances	Unwilling to try foods Upset by strong smells

helps children cope with gravity. A poor vestibular sense is present in dyslexia and dyspraxia.

Poor vestibular sense

The following list gives difficulties or observation points indicating a poor vestibular sense:

- a poor sense of balance;
- motion sickness;
- dislike of quick changes of direction;
- avoidance of equipment such as a climbing frame;
- being easily disoriented (hence, keep the environment calm and unflustered);
- bumping and dropping things;
- difficulty in staying still.

The kinaesthetic and proprioceptive senses

Although these two names are often used interchangeably, the kinaesthetic sense only comes into play when the body is moving, whereas the proprioceptive sense works all the time to relay positional information.

The proprioceptors are all over the body: in the skin, muscles and joints (receptors are even located in the hair follicles), and they literally tell us where we end and the outside world begins. So children with a poor proprioceptive sense often have difficulty in keeping still – they have to move so that their kinaesthetic and proprioceptive senses provide them with more secure information about where they are in space.

Poor kinaesthetic or proprioceptive sense

The following list gives difficulties or observation points indicating a poor kinaesthetic or proprioceptive sense:

- a poor sense of poise, e.g. the child who slumps over the table at craftwork or 'folds' when sitting on the floor at story time;
- easily tired by the constant effort needed to stay erect;
- constant movement and fidgeting (provide a beanbag to sit on and something to squeeze);
- poor depth perception, e.g. in misjudging the depth of stairs;
- poor sense of direction (rehearse 'where to go' ahead of the child having to do so independently);
- poor body awareness (play 'Simon says' types of games; for ideas see *Jingle Time*, Macintyre, 2003).

The visual sense

Assessing vision should cover much more than reading/distance vision that is often the main concern in a simple eye test. Children who 'pass' this can still have difficulties in *tracking*, i.e. following the words on a page or the writing on the board. Functional vision depends on maturation of the central nervous system. Visual-motor integration skills are also very important: the two eyes have to work together to focus on an image (*convergence*). Some children with poor convergence see double images that confuse letter recognition; others will see the letters move on the page and may endure severe eye strain trying to adjust to the movement. This is known as Mears-Irlen syndrome and can be helped by coloured overlays or coloured lenses in spectacles. Children also benefit from being allowed to choose the colour of paper that suits them best, for different colours cut out light reflection.

Children must also be able to adjust their focus so that they can decipher objects and print from different angles and directions. This is called *accommodation*. The three skills – convergence, accommodation and tracking

– are all prerequisites for quick identification and reading fluently without strain.

Poor visual sense

The following list gives difficulties or observation points indicating a poor visual sense:

- poor tracking skills;
- child saying that letters jump or overlap on the page;
- rubbing eyes or partially closing them to keep out the light;
- distress at being asked to choose a book.

The auditory sense

During the first three years, the child listens to and learns to tune in to sounds of their mother tongue. Thereafter, it is harder to adjust to the sounds of another language. Obviously, loss of hearing significantly affects learning, but children who 'can hear' may have auditory discrimination problems and these may be the basis of a recognised additional learning need, e.g. dyslexia or dyspraxia. If children cannot hear the difference between 'p' and 'b' or 'sh' and 'th', both reading and spelling will be impaired. Even silent reading is affected because children listen to an inner voice – if the sounds are not clear, this process will be affected in the same way as in reading aloud.

Hearing too much (i.e. auditory hypersensitivity) can cause as much difficulty as not hearing enough. Children bombarded by sound can have difficulty selecting what they need to hear from the variety of different noises around them. Even in a quiet classroom, some children find hearing the teacher difficult, as they cannot cut out minor rustles and squeaks.

Poor auditory sense

The following list gives difficulties or observation points indicating a poor auditory sense:

- oversensitive to sounds;
- confusion in distinguishing sounds;
- delay in responding;
- constantly asking for things to be repeated.

35

The tactile sense

Tactility or sensitivity to touch is important in feeding, in communicating and in generally feeling secure. Touch is one of the earliest sources of learning, and touch receptors cover the whole body. They are linked to a headband in the brain: the somatosensory cortex, which registers heat, cold, pressure, pain and body position. It makes an important contribution to the sense of balance.

Some children have a system that is overreactive to touch, and this causes them to be distressed by responses that most children welcome, such as hugs. This can make them isolated especially because families can mistakenly interpret their reactions as rejection. Yet these same children can be 'touchers' seeking out sensory stimulation through contacting others, even though they themselves would be distressed by such overtures.

Pain receptors can cause difficulties too. Some children are hyposensitive and may not feel pain or temperature change. They may tolerate holding hot plates or go out of doors without dressing for protection against icy winds. And the hypersensitive ones will overreact to injections and visits to the dentist because they feel so much pain. Some children feel pain even when having their nails or hair cut. All kinds of problems arise from being hypo- or hyper-touch-sensitive.

Poor tactile sense

The following list gives difficulties or observation points indicating a poor tactile sense:

- dislike of being touched, so withdrawing from contact;
- compulsively touching others;
- pain may cause over- or under-reaction;
- poor temperature control;
- allergies – possibly eczema;
- dislike of contact sports/games;
- if the child lacks protective control, he may not sense danger.

The senses of smell and touch

The sense of smell is the most evocative of the senses as it can stimulate memories, e.g. of a hot summer when the milk turned sour. The sense of smell can also stimulate the hormones controlling appetite, temperature and sexuality. Certain smells can become associated with different situations, e.g. the smell of a hospital can conjure up memories of pain, or the scent of flowers can recall a happy event such as a wedding, or a sad one such as a funeral.

The sense of taste depends on the sense of smell, so it is not difficult to understand why children refuse to accept new foods simply because they do not like the appearance or the smell. Some of the earliest learning comes through these senses; as we know, during the sensorimotor period, the baby will put everything to the mouth. This most sensitive part of the body will tell them about the taste and texture of the object and whether it is hard, soft or malleable, as well as whether the taste is pleasant or not.

Poor sense of taste and smell

The following list gives difficulties or observation points indicating a poor sense of taste or smell:

- children may be very fussy about new foods and only tolerate a very restricted diet;
- they may refuse to go to the bathroom because of the smell of antiseptics or even of scented soap;
- they may dislike being near other people especially if they wear perfume or aftershave.

SENSORY INTEGRATION

When children appear distressed it is vital to consider that their sensory input may be 'hyper' or 'hypo', i.e. giving too much input or too little. The child who bangs and crashes may not be receiving the signals that would allow him to cope in a gentler way. On the other hand, even a flickering light or a rustle may cause a sensitive child to be upset. Some children can explain what is wrong, but others, especially those on the autistic spectrum, will think you are already aware of their problems and fail to explain. Unfortunately, they may believe that nothing can be done. But practitioners can take steps so that the learning environment compensates for sensory difficulties.

Chapter 3

Understanding social development

When nursery practitioners are asked about the most important things they want their children to be able to do, it is likely that they will suggest at least some of the social items in the following list and select nursery activities that require planning, discussing, interacting and decision-making.

The group of practitioners named below appeared confident in identifying the social competences they were trying to instil in their young learners (see Table 3.1; other social skills are discussed below under

FIGURE 3.1 After studying some books on design, Anna and Sophie are sharing their ideas and co-operating to produce wallpaper patterns to decorate the house corner

■ TABLE 3.1 Some social skills

Respecting each other and the toys and other resources they have to play with (**Simon**)	Being kind to one another (**Sally**) Learning to take turns (**Amy**) Caring and sharing (**Megan**)
Learning to watch out for one another – to be aware of safety issues, especially when playing outside (**Carol**)	Learning to be independent by deciding what they want to do, gathering all the things they need and getting on with it (**Jo**)
Learning to cope when they get bumped or when pieces of work disappoint them (**Dave**)	Listening to each other and following another's lead (**Amy**)
Coping with the routine of the day – knowing what comes next (**Omar**)	Having a friend and being able to share that friend with others (**Fran**)

(The practitioners' names, in brackets, are given to ease referring back to the list).

'Understanding emotional development', pp. 59–74), although, in discussion, they had different views on how they might best be achieved. Enjoy the debate and add to the list if you can.

In a group discussion about children's development, this group of nursery nurses identified 'social development' as the most important aspect. However, they all nodded when Amy volunteered, 'they [i.e. all the aspects of development] overlap anyway and it's often difficult to differentiate, particularly between social and emotional'. They then answered the following questions.

Q Why should social development take priority?

Well, social skills are the stepping stones if you like – if you can trust children not to hit each other and share the resources without squabbling and breaking them, then you have time to concentrate on teaching them something, but if you have to stop fights and bickering all the time, then nothing gets done. (**Simon**)

Q How do you establish this kind of working atmosphere?

We try to act as role models, keeping calm and praising those who are behaving well. We hope the others will copy them. If they don't, then explaining why you are upset or disappointed is always better than being cross. **(Sally)**

Q What should you do if children already have good social skills? Should you develop these further or concentrate on other aspects of their development?

Even if some children appear to have developed sophisticated social skills, there are always ways to take their understanding forward. Jo was anxious to share her thoughts. She explained,

> We have a boy, Odie, who comes from what we would say was a disadvantaged background if we only thought about material things, but socially, he is tops! Despite some language difficulties, he has learned how to make friends with many of the others. He is always beaming and that's attractive, but he is respectful too. He listens to the other children and will offer to help them without being pushy. Sometimes he gets teased, but he doesn't retaliate as most youngsters would. He doesn't appear distressed either. I heard him say to another boy, 'Wouldn't it be dull if everyone looked exactly the same?' and I thought 'I must remember that and use it when we talk about different animals or even shapes of flowers and leaves.' We learn from the children all the time.

Q But what can Jo do to extend Odie's social learning?

> I give him responsible jobs like checking the equipment to make it ready for another child who has cerebral palsy. He fixes toys onto the slatted table and makes sure all the straps on the walking frame are in place.
>
> We have also asked Odie to say one or two phrases in Arabic so that the other children can learn them, realise that there are other languages and respect his bilingualism. We have a Welsh child too and one who has volunteered to teach us Gaelic so we are truly learning about different ways of communicating. It's important to make all children feel they can contribute to the curriculum.

Q I've found that some children start off being socially strong, but soon they follow the rougher children and copy their behaviour. This is very disappointing as we try to explain the best way to behave.

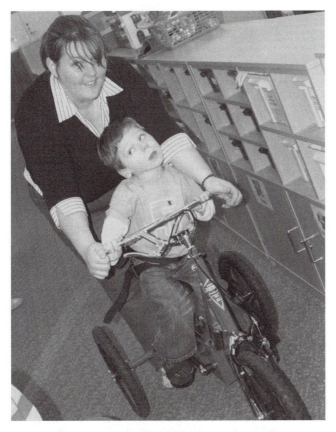

FIGURE 3.2 Jo helps Daniel's feeling of independence

At this point Dave interrupted,

> I've tried explaining what is acceptable behaviour over and over
> again. Sometimes giving rewards works for a short time, but often
> the children forget or don't seem to realise that looking out for
> others applies to everyone in the nursery all of the time.

He explained that chipping away at unacceptable behaviour was endlessly
repetitive and totally exhausting. Pressed to give an example, he went on,

> Ben is a well-built 4-year-old who bubbles with energy. Last week on
> Monday and Tuesday it was so wet that the children didn't get out

to play, so on Wednesday when Ben saw the bikes come out, he rushed to the door crashing the area partitions over as he went. Lia was in his way so he just pushed her as hard as he could and she fell into the box of building equipment, bruising her back. As she was marked as well as distressed we had to record the incident and tell Ben's Mum. When we did, she grabbed Ben's jersey and marched him up to Lia. 'Did he hit you?' she asked. Lia nodded shyly. 'Well, belt him back!' she was told. Lia cowered back. 'Come on, get your own back,' she went on, 'or I'll do it for you.'

The group agreed that these sorts of incidents concerned them deeply. They felt totally at a loss when home 'rules' conflicted with the caring philosophy of the nursery. They were also aware that Ben's Mum's parting shot had been: 'Namby-pamby's no use out in the real world. That kid'll not survive if she doesn't hit back. It's a jungle out there!'

These children have to adapt to both home ways and nursery ways. 'At least in nursery, they learn there's an alternative way to behave,' claimed Dave, 'but what do we do when we get told, "My Dad says, 'If he hits you, hit him back twice as hard and he'll not do it again'"?'

This is not an easy problem to resolve, as, while the nursery can't be seen to criticise the home, the parents or caregivers have to agree that in nursery, the nursery social rules must apply. Talking with the parents, calmly explaining 'this is what we do' and sending a leaflet home illustrating instances of good behaviour are useful steps. It is also a good idea to record what was done in a diary in case of later retributions. In extreme cases, e.g. when the parents or caregivers absolutely reject behaviour policies, they can be reminded that they are free to remove their child from nursery care.

ESTABLISHING NURSERY 'RULES'

Q Jo asked, 'Should we not take a much more proactive approach?' She explained:

When issues like this arise, we get the parents in and just tell them that we don't allow physical retaliation. Before that, of course, we would know whether a child's outburst was a one-off, or if it was his usual way of behaving. We would also have made sure we had tried to recognise any difficulties, e.g. frustration caused by poor language, that were causing the problem. But both parents and

children, and all of the staff, have to show that they agree with
nursery policies – it's the only way to have a stable environment.

Jo also found that some children played the staff off one against another,
'They'll hassle different members of staff till they get their own way,'
she claimed. 'We have to know we are sticking to the same rules!'

Sally, whose ideal was that the children should learn to care for one
another, added her thoughts. She explained:

> The reality is that the children have to learn two sets of rules, just
> like having one language for the playground and another for inside
> school. Unfortunately, many of the Playstation games and even
> television programmes present bullies as the stars. And the
> children watch them all the time. What kind of message is that?

The group nodded total agreement but felt powerless to make any change.
Simon added,

> But children have always liked blood and thunder, yet they knew it
> wasn't real. Why should this be different now?

Debates about what encourages violent behaviour rage on.

Q **Dave was anxious to consider the layout of the nursery itself.
He asked: 'Could the arrangement of the tables in the
nursery contribute to rowdy behaviour? I think you have
to look at the pathways around the tables and not have long
runs because they encourage the children to charge around.
Perhaps this is what caused Ben to lose control?'**

> [Sally replied:] It's quite complicated to get the best arrangement
> because of access to the fire door and keeping the cooking area
> separate. Then there's the water tray. It's easiest if that's near
> the taps and the sand area can't be near the carpet. But I've just
> thought of a long run in our setting and I think it does encourage
> charging, so I'll rethink the layout and see if that helps.

HELPING THE CHILDREN UNDERSTAND SOCIAL 'RULES'

Nursery staff know that, in their homes, children have different sets of
rules. Indeed, some appear to have none or a set that changes from day

to day or from person to person, leaving the children totally confused as to how to behave in different situations. How do practitioners begin to help them accept stability and consistency?

Fran explained:

> The first message we try to establish is, 'In the nursery we are all friends' and although the children can't read, we have a large notice pinned up with pictures of smiling babies, toddlers and pre-schoolers with the words underneath. Every day at one point we repeat this like a mantra! Then we discuss what a friend is. The children learn that it's someone who is kind, who lets you play and helps you with your coat. It is someone who speaks quietly and plays gently.
>
> We let the children know we are looking out for children who behave like that and when they do we will praise them or give them a sticker. These work wonders, especially when they can take them home to show they've been good.

FIGURE 3.3 Orla and Fin work together in the garden; their interest in growing things means they are best friends

UNDERSTANDING AGGRESSION IN YOUNG CHILDREN

Aggression is behaviour with the intent to harm another person, and most children will show some form of aggression in the early years, possibly because they have not yet learned to appreciate what another person is feeling (see the development of a theory of mind in 'Understanding emotional development', pp. 59–74). In the early years, aggressive behaviour (e.g. grabbing a toy from a sibling) can be reinforced by finding that this is what works. The aggression enables the child to get the toy and this may be much more important to him than the scolding that will follow. Fortunately, aggression does tend to diminish in frequency as verbal skills improve (see Table 3.2).

Table 3.2 shows that as early as the ages of 3 or 4 dominance hierarchies come into play. Even at this early age, children understand pecking orders of leaders and followers. They know who will win a fight, which children they dare attack, and which they must avoid. This can help counter physical aggression.

TABLE 3.2 Changes in patterns of aggression

Changes in the type of aggression	Children aged 2–4	Children aged 4–8
Physical aggression – e.g. biting, hitting, pushing	Most often used at this stage	Getting less
Verbal aggression – e.g. name calling, taunting	Not often used at 2; this increases as effects are recognised and language skills improve	Most often used at this age when 'rules' about hitting and biting are internalised
The reason why	Instrumental aggression aiming to procure something or to break something	The aim is to show power or to hurt feelings or humiliate another person
Why does it happen?	Frustration – often after being denied something	Competitive instinct emerging
After effects	Short lived, but bullying can emerge	Longer lasting hurt influenced by amount of support and temperament of the child

At this point, the group debated the need for rewards for good behaviour, i.e. what should be the 'norm' and the conclusion was that, for a short time, rewards such as stickers, even home-made ones, were helpful for children who had to make real adjustments in their behaviour.

Q **I agree that stickers encourage individuals, but what could we do to explain appropriate social behaviour to a larger group? This would prevent the 'endless chipping away' (the repetition) that is so frustrating?**

Fran volunteered another suggestion. She explained:

> In the nursery, acting out a story with puppets is one way to show different ways of behaving. The puppets become the goodies and the baddies, and children both hear and see the results of how they behave. In one story about getting to join in a game, one puppet can be aggressive, perhaps jumping up and down shouting out 'Let me in!' while another quietly asks 'Can I play?' The first puppet is told, 'No', while the second is welcomed into the game. The children can then share their thoughts, and soon the children appreciate why some children are chosen as friends. In other words, they learn what makes children popular.

POPULAR AND REJECTED CHILDREN

Q **But why should some children be popular while others are neglected or rejected?**

It is particularly important to understand these characteristics, as they seem to be relatively stable over time. Popular children are those other children choose to play with or work with, while the 'neglected' ones are tolerated without much enthusiasm. They are not actively disliked but are not sought out as friends. Sadly, the rejected ones are left isolated or openly taunted, despite the best efforts of adults urging other children to 'let them play'.

Making children aware of these characteristics could be a positive move if it enabled children to reflect and change their behaviour. While this is what education is trying to do, so many variables, e.g. the child's temperament, social background, disability and, in the early stages, physical appearance, impinge and make this change much more complex than it would appear to be at first glance. If we link these characteristics with

▉ TABLE 3.3 Characteristics of popular, neglected and rejected children

Popular children tend to	Neglected children	Rejected children tend to
Be physically larger	Can't do physical tasks which others see as important, e.g. riding a bike, kicking a ball	Tell tales, complaining to adults
Be attractive, with striking physical features such as long hair	Are ordinary or average children without particular social skills; Are too clever and boastful about their own abilities	Be different in some way – even ways that are beyond their control, e.g. having physical features that others find displeasing; very overweight children
Have a 'cool' dress sense	Lack 'street cred'	Sometimes be untidy or dirty
Behave kindly to others (crucial)	Are not consistent so other children are less sure how to communicate	Join other rejected children but with a bad grace
Be good at explaining – non-punitive	Are unsure how to fit in	Have a short fuse – will hit out or tell tales
Stay loyal to friends; consistent in the way they respond	Flit from group to group; pine to be included	Become withdrawn and/or resentful
Stay calm and rational	Are unpredictable	Be surly, unpleasant children

the enduring temperamental traits explained in Chapter 1, the interaction of nature and nurture appears once more. Moreover, it is not difficult to imagine the impact on the child's self-esteem when they recognise that they are not well liked (see 'Understanding emotional development', pp. 59–74).

WHERE DOES IT ALL BEGIN? HOW DO CHILDREN DEVELOP SOCIAL SKILLS?

Bowlby (1988) and Ainsworth (1972) are key researchers into the formation and importance of attachment or bonding between parents and their children. Bowlby argues that 'the propensity to make strong emotional bonds to particular individuals is a basic component of human nature, already present in the neonate'. He shows that this early relationship is sustained by the infant being fed and by the interplay of communicative behaviours, e.g. cooing, stroking and smiling. The baby forms an attachment based on the sense of security that develops.

This research has had a profound effect on birth practices; fathers were suddenly expected to be present at the birth rather than pacing in the waiting room, so that they could share this bonding experience. Myers (1999), however, has cast doubt on the immediacy of this.

This must be a great comfort to parents whose children have had to be in intensive care or where 'the baby blues' prevented mothers from expressing warm feelings in the first days or even weeks after giving birth. The strength of the bonding is now thought to depend on the pattern of interlocking attachment behaviours that develop over the first weeks and months. As the babies and parents learn about each other they are building up a repertoire of behaviours that they know will please the other. They are fostering communication and mutuality. This is called synchrony and it takes families different lengths of time to achieve. It is fostered by cuddling, talking to the baby and encouraging/smiling at the baby's responses so that each party in the duo learns what pleases the other. A father's skills are very similar to those of the mother and so the caregivers should complement one another, allowing the baby to build two secure bonds.

But does this always happen? Sometimes parents of very premature babies are afraid to bond, fearing great distress should the baby die. Babies on ventilators and feeding tubes cannot be held, and, when they do go home, the responsibility can cause such tension and tiredness that parents can feel anguish rather than love. But usually this passes – there is time for things to settle down and for all to be well. Parents with a difficult baby, however, may feel they are underachieving, even failing, if they do not meet 'society's expectations', whatever they may be. Some parents can be disappointed in their child, especially if there is a disability, and this can be very hard to overcome. Other mothers may lack the experience of a secure and loving environment themselves; they may not have the support of the father, or enough money to cope; and, if at the end of their tether, they may abuse the child. One very young mother explained, 'I just wanted someone to love me but she didn't. She just cried all the time and in the end I hit her. I was desperate for someone to take her away and let me sleep. Yet all the time I was overwhelmed by feeling guilty too. Why did nobody tell me it would be like this?' Why indeed? Perhaps we are letting our adolescents down by not pointing out the worries of parenthood as well as the pleasures.

Happily, however, most early traumas are resolved and the attachment that is formed can last throughout life, providing mutual support for those involved. The importance of this cannot be overstated. As Schaffer (1990) claims: 'the establishment of the child's primary social relationships is the foundation on which all psychosocial behaviour is based.' He also claimed 'any early break will have long lasting effects'.

Many children have breaks of one kind or another through hospital-isation, family breakdown and going to a childminder or nursery. Research has discovered that before 7 months old, children would settle happily with others: the children were interested rather than alarmed by their changed surroundings. But after that, the babies' responses were to cry and cling and show signs of distress. This is the classic separation effect, when children will show lengthy periods of being unsettled with their sleep patterns destroyed. The timing of bonding for the children (rather than the parents) has been judged from findings such as this.

So what happens when children go to childminders/nursery at age 2 or 3 years? If the second setting is similar to the first and shows 'con-tingent responsiveness', i.e. the new caregiver responds with smiles and reassurance, then the child has a second secure base and this need not affect the attachment to the first. But where discrepancies in child-rearing practices are found, then the more vulnerable children are left with a sense of anomie, i.e. disquiet and insecurity. These findings remained constant after researchers controlled for variables such as social class. The effect of being securely or insecurely attached can last at least into adolescence. Research also found that securely attached babies became more confident youngsters; they were anxious to be involved in more activities and they had a greater sense of their own ability to accomplish things. A bonus indeed!

Melhuish (1990) compared the progress of children who experienced care with relatives, childminding or private nursery care. He found that children in nurseries received less language stimulation, possibly because of the reduced adult:child ratio. There were few differences in cognitive development but in social development the nurseries shone. The children there showed more pro-social behaviour such as sharing and co-operating with others.

SOCIAL INFLUENCES ON THE FAMILY

The specific family environment also has profound effects. The ideal environment is one where the caregivers have good interaction skills and respond appropriately to the children's cues. The children also need resources to stimulate their potential for investigating, although these need not be expensive. At the other end of the scale, some families cannot provide even the most basic comforts and the children are brought up amid chaos and despair. There are many shades of care on this continuum, so it is no surprise that children come to nursery with very different views of what the new experience will hold and very different ideas of what kind of behaviour will win favour or displeasure in that setting.

The family, of course, is embedded in a much larger social structure, i.e. a community, which has its own economic, social and cultural system. Infants in poor communities may be exposed to environmental toxins; they may be less likely to have immunisations and regular health care; and they may have nutritionally suspect diets. The differences in the children's backgrounds can become apparent at ages 2, 3 or 4. One remedy is to provide social support for parents in the poverty trap. Single parents may never have a break and they are more likely to have a crying, distressed child. Providing a meeting place in nursery for mothers and fathers on a regular basis can mean that the children benefit from a release of the tensions brought on by isolation.

HEALTH IN THE PRE-SCHOOL YEARS

Acute illnesses such as brief bouts of sickness or streaming colds are common in the first years. Children living in more stressful settings have greater health vulnerability and this can place immense social strain on caregivers, who must make themselves absent from work in order to care for the children. The majority of accidents also occur at home and are more usual for boys than girls.

Finally for this section, Eisenberg (1990) advises us what to do if we want to rear helpful children:

1   create a warm and loving family climate;
2   explain why and give clear rules about what to do as well as what not to do;
3   provide pro-social positive feedback, e.g. 'you are such a helpful child';

4   give children opportunities to do helpful things;
5   demonstrate thoughtful and generous behaviour.

And when we read these things, we find that the nursery staff group at the start of the chapter had provided a sound set of competences too.

Q In March 2006, the press reported that one mother was suing the school for suspending her 4-year-old for bullying! So despite all the work on developing social skills, is the reality that bullying in the nursery must happen?

KEY TOPIC

Bullying in the nursery

You are really asking whether very young children bully? This is not an easy question. If the answer is 'yes', what sorts of things do they do? And if the answer is 'no', then what causes some of them to start, for despite everyone's efforts to stop bullying, it is still endemic across all social groups and all age groups.

Q Does it not depend on what you think bullying is?

Let's begin by reflecting on the children and the experiences they encounter. First of all, who are the children who share early years education?

They are a group of very young people of different ages (and remember that one year could mean one-third of a child's lifespan at that sort of age.) and different developmental stages (some of the 3-year-olds may be more able than the 4-year-olds). They are of different shapes, sizes, colours, intellectual abilities, social competences, movement skills and emotional stabilities. Some will have the expressive language to share their needs, or will have the articulation or understanding of the nuances of language to use the spoken word – and some will not. They will have different temperaments – there are easy-going, confident and creative children, acutely anxious children, slow to warm-up children and those who will not or cannot wait. They have come from hugely varied backgrounds with different home and out-of-school experiences, different levels of common sense, and different cultural beliefs. Is it any wonder that when we group all of them together in a confined space, some children, possibly attempting to gain status and make themselves heard, resort to bullying?

51

To add to the complexity, interest and challenge of managing these children, they are not passive learners waiting to hear the practitioners' words of wisdom and advice. They come into a new situation with different expectations of what will be there, how important it will be and what they will do to cope. Some will even recognise that people at home have expectations of them too. They have different experiences of being parented, they have learned different 'rules', e.g. whether to retaliate when they are upset, and how to do it. Some will be trained to look after resources and accept that it is their job to tidy up. Others will rebel when a non-family adult tells them what to do or decides what kinds of food they should have at snack time. The differences between home rules and nursery rules can be very confusing. The children also have different levels of financial backing, home resources and support, and, to some extent, this colours their perception of their new environment.

Q Given, then, that there are all these differences, how do children adapt to the early years setting? What things do these children have to learn?

- that they will be safe;
- how to follow a complex routine;
- how to make a friend;
- how to take turns – to wait – to deal with delayed gratification;
- how to relate to 'strange' adults and other children who may not behave the way they do;
- how to be still and listen to others;
- how to climb on a climbing frame and ride a bike outside;
- how to deal with praise and disappointment;
- how to cut out distractions and concentrate;
- how to do all the activities and tasks.

Above all, the children have to learn to respect themselves and the other children, the adults who care for them, and the resources that are provided. This takes different lengths of time depending on the willingness of the child to conform and the coherence or conflict between the child's previous experiences and this new one.

Q I'd like to think about the setting again. Can it affect the less-confident children because they are the ones who get bullied? What can be done?

All of the intrinsic differences already mentioned are brought together in a setting which in itself may be frightening, e.g. toilets that flush noisily. (A practitioner in one setting, proud of the new self-flushing loos, was dismayed that no one would go in. It was discovered that one child had suggested a ghost was flushing them.) There are also bells that ring and radiators that buzz, walls that have too many confusing pictures, lights that flicker and doors that have double locks. 'Who needs to be kept out?' asked one fearful child. Even the large floor space can be frightening, especially if noise reverberates off the floors.

Q How do we identify bullying behaviour?

Bullying behaviour is 'persistent, intentional, conscious cruelty, perpetrated against those who are unable to defend themselves' (Murray and Keene 1998). We would hope that not many nursery age children would persist in harming the same child. But it does happen.

Q Who are the children most likely to be bullied?

The group of practitioners made this list:

- Fragile children, e.g. small, slightly built children who don't meet the criterion of 'being big'.
- Vulnerable children, e.g. those who are different in some way: different skin colour, cultural practices, clothing or any other feature that makes the child stand out from the rest.
- Disabled children, especially those who have a hidden disability (e.g. dyspraxia, ADHD or Asperger's syndrome) because their difficulties are not immediately apparent and the children don't understand why they bump all the time or make loud noises or don't respond to their overtures in the usual way. It is interesting that often children with obvious differences, e.g. those with Down's syndrome, will be nurtured, showing that compassion can be aroused in most children. Sadly however, hurtful name-calling can affect them too.
- The most able children who know all the answers and converse in more adult ways.
- All those who can't or won't retaliate.

53

Q Do you find that making children aware of the effects of bullying makes them stop?

Hopefully, pointing out the hurt that bullying causes will make all children stop and think twice about bullying behaviour, but sadly this is not guaranteed. Murray and Keene (1998) found: 'While children say they abhor the practice of bullying, many children claim it pays off, because if they intimidate others, then that stops them being bullied themselves.'

Q Why does bullying happen?

For any reason or for no reason at all.

Q What numbers are we talking about?

The list is frightening.

- 20 per cent of children are afraid to go to school;
- 38 per cent of primary school age children report they have been distressed to the extent that their lifestyle has been harmed;
- 15 per cent of women are affected by sexual bullying;
- 15 per cent of men are bullied at work;
- 25 per cent of adults, even old people, suffer physical and/or verbal abuse;
- 14 per cent of suicides are associated with bullying.

It can clearly be seen that bullying causes enormous hurt and damage that can last for a lifetime, or even cause a life to be extinguished. It is continual nastiness – real or even imagined, for the anticipation can be as overwhelming as the incidents themselves.

Q Is there a gender difference? Do boys and girls use the same techniques?

See Table 3.4 for a summary of information.

The gender difference is apparent even at 4 years old. Girls are much more likely to use relational aggression (e.g. 'I'll get my Daddy onto you – he's a policeman') or bribery (e.g. 'I won't ask you to my party

TABLE 3.4 Gender differences in bullying techniques (in per cent)

Type of behaviour	Boys	Girls
Mean to others	21.8	9.6
Physical attacks	18.1	4.4
Gets involved in many fights	30.9	9.8
Destroys things belonging to others	10.6	4.4
Destroys self/own possessions	10.7	2.1

Source: Adapted from Bee, 2002, after Cummings *et al.*, 1986, Goodenough, 1931 and Hartup, 1974.

unless . . .'). Or they make sly faces. It is also revealing to note that girls tend to bully other girls; and they are also likely to run to an adult to complain.

Boys, on the other hand, tend to use physical aggression but, in contrast, appear to get less emotionally involved. They see bullying as par for the course, something that has to be expected and accepted. They either hit back or crumple but tend not to 'tell' until things have escalated; and of course the difficulties for both bully and victim are then more entrenched.

These differences show that there are different types of bullies depending on the innate characteristics of the child, e.g. their temperament and/or the environmental/cultural experiences they have had.

Q Does the type of bullying stay the same?

The type of behaviour used does change over time – from the overt physical abuse in the early years to the hidden, sly innuendoes later on. The variety of bullying behaviour increases, yet incidents can be difficult to describe, and can sound petty in the retelling. This is what makes it so hard for children to explain, and holds them back from sharing their fears. There is also the implicit fear that their own inadequacy may be to blame.

DIFFERENT TYPES OF BULLIES

It is important to distinguish between the different types of bullying because therein lies a clue to giving the most appropriate kind of support.

Reactive bullies

These are children who have experienced significant hurt or been overwhelmed by events either inside nursery/school or at home. Divorce, bereavement, even a best friend moving away may be the cause. The children lash out in frustration at their inability to remedy the situation.

Anxious bullies

These are the children who show deep-seated insecurity and they attempt to gain status through bullying. This may be a self-preservation mechanism.

Both of these need support and positive feedback. They are usually willing to listen and evaluate their actions if these are explained in a non-judgemental way.

Sadistic bullies

In contrast, there are sadistic bullies who show no regard for others' feelings. They mock any attempt to reason. They defy parents and teachers. They seem to enjoy inflicting pain. They have no altruism or empathy – they become the 'hard nut' bullies and may eventually find that only other children of like minds will tolerate them as 'friends'. In this way gangs are formed. They don't appear to care for their own well-being, or for that of others. They may have a conduct disorder, e.g. OBD (oppositional behaviour disorder) or ADHD, i.e. a neurobiological disorder requiring medical attention.

It can be hard for these children to accept that they do need help and they will usually deny that change is required. They cause resentment and many parents and teachers, after they have tried all the positive approaches, want them to be excluded from school as they disrupt learning for all the other children and may cause physical and emotional harm.

DIFFERENT KINDS OF ABUSE

The difficulty in 'sorting things out' can often lie in the fact that the type of behaviour can vary from day to day – so the 'I promise not to hide Marie's shoes again' (making her really anxious and upset) is easily kept, while at the same time another form of aggression is substituted for it. 'Not knowing what the bully will do next' can cause the victim to live in fear for the whole day.

There is also the issue that it can be the *way* the taunt is delivered, rather than the words themselves, that can hurt; and when these are repeated in another context, they can seem innocuous. It's often not what is said, but the way it's said, that is the problem. However, the list is endless and possibilities increase when there is less or no adult supervision. In the primary years, the playground and the area outside the school gates (where adults do not see what is going on) are often greatly feared.

PARENTS' RESPONSES

It is hugely distressing for the parents to know that their child is the victim of bullying. A first understandable reaction might be: 'What can I do? I wasn't there. I didn't see what was going on.' But others may react differently. They may:

- not know what to do and hope it will go away: 'they'll be onto someone else next week';
- brush their child's worries aside: 'I was bullied too – you just have to put up with it';
- blame the school for letting it happen: 'Wait till I get down there – they should be on top of bullying by now';
- blame their child for not coping: 'For goodness sake, wise up and stand up for yourself';
- encourage the child to retaliate: 'If he hits you, hit him back twice as hard and he won't bother you again';
- ask the bully home to see what the reaction is in the child's home setting: 'Let's see if you can be friends';
- tackle the bully themselves or tackle the bully's parents (who may or may not be aware of what is going on): 'Right, I'll sort this if no one else will';
- feel powerless, especially if there is no obvious evidence, e.g. scratches, bruises, or items being stolen.

It is not difficult to understand why parents can be confused and reluctant to act, especially if their child begs them not to interfere in case of more reprisals from the bullies, or if the staff tell them they're overreacting. Fortunately, schools have clearly laid out policies for dealing with bullying – but it still goes on.

In the early years, staff usually have more opportunities to meet the parents and build the kind of relationship that allows honest interaction.

They can confirm that the practitioners will do everything in their power to wipe out inappropriate behaviour so that each child can learn peacefully. This done, the parents can recognise that the early years setting is the very best place for their child to be and they can co-operate in eliminating aggressive behaviour.

Chapter 4

Understanding emotional development

While social skills enable children to interact with other adults and children in the nursery in an age-related way, they are dependent on a number of emotional competences that work to let children know who they are and who others are. There is a sequence of development which is partly down to nature (e.g. the maturational unfolding of emotional competences) and partly down to nurture (e.g. the experiences and opportunities the children have and the role models which provide examples of behaviour and set cultural mores). During this process, the children begin to make comparisons and evaluations and this helps them form their self-concept. At this point Jacki said she was confused.

Q If I think about children learning to share, then that is part of social development, isn't it? What sorts of underlying attitudes make social observations like these into emotional ones?

If we were considering emotional development, then we would want to know the reasoning behind what the children do. So children learning to share, move beyond instrumental reasons: for example, 'I'd better do this because it's what I'm expected to do and it might earn me a sticker', changes to 'If I give someone else this toy then they will feel happier, even though I want it myself'. This is the development of altruism, i.e. doing something for someone else at some cost to oneself. So when we are considering emotional development, we have to pull apart the overt social acts to find what kind of understanding is being shown. Practitioners need to know how that understanding develops.

FIGURE 4.1
Sindhu is learning
about caring
for others and
developing altruism

Q When do children develop a sense of self? When do they have a clear picture of who they are and understand that other people have different attitudes, priorities and ideas about behaviour? How do they learn to respect different points of view? When children call out 'It's not fair', do they understand the concept of fairness, or is this just a cry that they hope will get them what they want? And if they are fair to others who then fail to reciprocate this behaviour, what then?

These are intriguing questions that really dig deep. They add a qualitative framework to social observations because they don't look only at the things children do but they aim to find out 'why they do them', and that shows the development of these subtle qualities. And if staff record examples of children showing these qualities, e.g. when one child admires another's drawing knowing that the praise will please the recipient, staff can record this as altruism. This is an important observation, because to give and receive praise is a definite example of both generosity and confidence. Perhaps recognising altruistic acts such as these can help us to make more of scenarios when opportunities to enhance children's emotional development arise.

TABLE 4.1 Some emotional competences

Know their own talents and needs and accept them – while aiming to improve	Realise that other children are less able and offer them support
Be fair to everyone else	Know how to make a friend
Have enough confidence to try new things	Be ready to praise others and praise themselves too
Tell other children they are good at something	Recognise feelings, e.g. of jealousy of a new baby, and know how to overcome them
Cope with anger in an acceptable way	Have a positive self-esteem
Understand that everyone has sad times – be compassionate to others when they are feeling upset	Be able to share thoughts and worries rather than bottling them up
Recognise what another person is thinking and respect that point of view	Understand what to do to comfort someone who gets hurt

The staff group were asked to put their heads together and identify some emotional competences. They produced the list shown in Table 4.1.

Table 4.1 shows a number of important developmental competences that may be hard to observe. But when should they appear? Is there an age-related developmental sequence? When does this begin?

DEVELOPING A SENSE OF SELF

Q You talked about a sense of self as a basis for children learning about their own selves and how they relate to others. But how do I know whether a child is developing it or not? Can I find this out when children are very young?

In his video, 'Play for tomorrow', Trevarthen demonstrates what he calls 'an ingenious experiment' to find if children recognise who they are. This is the first sign of a developing sense of self. This involves placing a dab of rouge on a child's nose then showing him his reflection in a mirror. The child of 3, 6, 9 and 14 months does not touch his nose because he does not know that the person he sees is himself, while the children of 2-plus do. They recognise that the reflections they see in the mirror are themselves. This is a necessary basis for making self-assessments and building comparisons between themselves and others. Many nurseries watch children enjoying their reflection in a mirror. But do they know whether they know the person there is themselves? Have they even a rudimentary sense of self? This simple test is a way to find out.

By 20 months, toddlers are beginning to understand that they are different from others. They know they have various properties, e.g. red hair, two hands and one nose. They can point to their own body parts and identify those same parts on others in picture books. This is a good way of promoting body awareness. At some time between 2 and 4 years, the children move beyond this and describe themselves by the skills they have achieved. For example, 'I can do a jigsaw'; 'I can ride a bike and tie my laces. I can paint and climb on the frame'. But these separate parts of the 'self-scheme' (or internal working model) the children have, do not yet blend into a model of self-worth. For this reason purists would not talk about nursery children as having 'a self-esteem'. While they can say, 'I am good at drawing', or singing or whatever, they don't build the separate achievements into a global whole. This happens at around age 7, when children begin to make judgements about what they see as their worth. This can colour their whole attitude to new learning: 'I'm good at that so I'll have a go', or 'I'll never be able to do that so I won't try' are often-heard cries. The children are reflecting on previous experiences and transferring these assessments to new opportunities. They are also involving themselves in deciphering how they appear to other people showing that they are developing a theory of mind. This is why it is so important that the children's first separate self-assessments are positive ones. They form the building blocks for their developing self-concept.

Q **What is the self-concept? It's a difficult term to understand. Why should some children have a more positive picture of themselves than others when they are much less able?**

The self-concept is the overarching picture children have of themselves, built in the process of growing up. Particularly in the early years, the picture fluctuates as different 'important people' show different reactions. These reactions are both verbal and, even more importantly, non-verbal. The children are evaluating these reactions and so building their self-concept. If they are accurate, then there will be a match with what others see, but the child may build a false picture and that surprises onlookers. So we can have an apparently precocious child, who considers themself to be smart and yet in reality lacks skills, and in contrast an able child who doesn't recognise their gifts at all.

KEY TOPIC

Enhancing the self-concept

It's a good idea to listen carefully to how children talk about themselves and so find what things are important to them. Pre-school children usually talk about visible characteristics, e.g. whether they are a boy or a girl, although some 4-year-olds can still be unsure of this. They will explain that they are 'big', or tell about where they live or all about their pet, i.e. concrete things, rather than whether they are brave or kind or clever, because these abstract concepts are still difficult for them to handle. They expect other people to know their pet's name and the relationships of everyone in their family photo, not appreciating that outsiders don't have the opportunities to know these things. This picture of themselves is influenced by people around them, particularly the significant others, i.e. parents, then teachers, then friends and heroes. If they are surrounded by smiling adults who have time to listen, encourage and play, then the picture is more likely to be a positive one. Even that can fluctuate when things go awry and induce self-doubt, or when illness makes the child weepy. But once these hurdles have been cleared, the positive self-concept should emerge again.

The opportunities children have to be independent and take risks influence this picture too. If children are overprotected or swamped by adults doing too much for them, they can develop 'learned helplessness', and lose the early intrinsic motivation to move and learn and cope. The self-concept picture gradually stabilises and early snapshots gradually become confirmed. This is why the early years settings have such an important part to play in determining children's long-lasting attitudes and self-beliefs.

THE EMERGING SELF-ESTEEM

Q Then there's the self-esteem. How does that differ from the self-concept?

The self-esteem is the evaluative part of the picture, i.e. the self-worth. Children gradually begin to be aware that others, both family and peers, are making comparisons and judging them, even reacting to them differently according to whether they are seen to be capable or attractive or not. These evaluations (i.e. ones deduced from the tridimensional image) may be mistaken because it is so difficult to read non-verbal cues accurately. But, nonetheless, children build a picture of themselves through imagining what these judgements are. This is the self-esteem.

THE IDEAL SELF

Later, when the children begin to admire others, they begin to compare their own self to that of their ideal self. The distance they perceive between the two colours their self-esteem. It can stimulate children to strive to achieve or, if they judge the distance to be unachievable, they may give up trying altogether. This sequence mirrors the stages children pass through in their intellectual or cognitive development.

Q How can we boost a child's self-esteem?

First of all, try to see things from the child's point of view. Most young children want to fit into their different environments and learn the kind of behaviour that is valued there. But sometimes children can find this difficult. If their names are called out time after time as people who are misbehaving, they might be hurt and withdraw, they might adopt a 'don't care' attitude, or they might ignore the correction altogether. This is why practitioners are urged to ignore minor misdemeanours as long as no other child is in danger of being hurt and to 'catch' the miscreants being good. It can be very revealing to tape a session and count just how many times one child's name is called out.

The general tenet is to give *lots of praise* – even for small things, as long as they are deserved. Children can usually detect false praise, but there will be something, even standing quietly, that deserves a positive mention. However, giving praise is not straightforward at all.

Giving praise

At first glance this would seem to be a simple matter of telling children they are good at something so that they build confidence in their own abilities. Unfortunately, this is not so. Children from age 3 or so are beginning to self-evaluate and make assessments for themselves. So telling them that they are proficient when they realise they're not is of little use. They recognise the truth. Certainly, children need to know that adults recognise their strengths, and fulsome praise is usually welcomed before the age when children assess their own capabilities. The move that 'all reporting home must be couched in positive terms' sprang from the realisation that negative assessments were of no use, and actually harmful. But parents know their children too. Perhaps saying what the child has achieved and then sharing a plan for development would be the best way. This could be the same for every child, the content differing for the stage of development and the individual profile of competences each child has.

A second important impact on emotional development lies in the way children are given praise. Many adults consider that public praise, when everyone stops to listen or look while the child is awarded a sticker or other reward, pleases every child. Not so. While every child likes to have their work acknowledged, many children prefer a quiet, private 'well done' or just an approving nod. They feel inhibited by public praise and may even limit their effort to avoid it.

Giving rewards

Similarly, giving rewards must be done with care. The early pleasure in gathering stickers does pass – although in the early years they still appear to be effective in promoting good behaviour. Later, however, children have their own preferences and these are the things that give most pleasure and so reinforce the child. It can be beneficial to ask the children what they would prefer rather than assume that you know. Children with autism certainly require to be asked. Sam (in *George and Sam*, Moore, 2004) chose a birthday treat of visiting launderettes to see the spinning drums and, while this is probably beyond the possibility for a nursery, Sam's other choice of sitting on a radiator for a time might well be managed. These 'treats' would not immediately be recognised as such by those who hadn't consulted the children.

DEVELOPMENT OF THE GENDER CONCEPT AND SEX ROLES

Q An important part of developing a sense of self must be gender related. When do boys and girls develop this sense and what difference does it make? In the early years we try to treat boys and girls the same. Is this OK?

Children gradually learn whether they are a boy or girl and that this state is permanent and doesn't change even when hairstyles alter or different clothes are worn. This is the *gender concept*. They then, through imitation and role-play, learn what behaviours are appropriate for that gender. These are *sex roles* and they are very different in different cultures, e.g. how girls are valued compared with boys and what roles they are expected to play. Nursery staff have to be very aware of these so that they can respect *each* child and don't inadvertently demean the children's cultural values and traditions. What makes this easier is the research finding that sex-role stereotypes are fairly consistent across the world. Researchers studied gender stereotypes in 28 countries and found that, even in 2004, they all described women as 'gentle, compassionate, tactful and expressive', while men were regarded as being 'competent, logical, assertive and able to get things done'. I wonder if some young children alter their behaviour, even feel pressurised to fit the mould? How stressful must this be?

Despite recent massive shifts in roles, e.g. two parents working or Dad staying home as a house-husband, 2-year-olds still appear to link Mums with vacuum cleaners and sinks. This endures even when Mums are out in the workplace holding down taxing jobs. One 4-year-old insisted all doctors were men, even though his mother was one. So, understanding these stereotypes is important: they provide one mode of entry into understanding the thoughts and behaviours of young children.

These ideas complement the parts children play in different social settings. They realise that they can be leaders or helpers or take different roles such as Mum or Dad or Doctor. This can be observed as children progress through the stages of play (solitary, parallel, co-operative, then socio-dramatic). And as they develop the understanding that they are boys or girls and have this stereotypical image in their heads, they begin to assign behaviours to different roles and question, for example, whether it is right that boys should play with dolls. Six-year-olds who were asked this replied: 'Well, it's not the same kind of wrong as stealing or hitting, but it's just not right somehow. People will laugh at you if you choose

FIGURE 4.2
Jake is enjoying the experience of being a dancer

the wrong things to play with.' Despite nurseries encouraging boys to dance and bake, somehow the two sexes themselves eventually allocate different preferences to each sex.

This may, of course, be reinforced at home. Even unspoken pats and smiles are strong communicators. These, plus developing interests, also explain why friendships start to be single sex, with boys choosing boys and girls, girls.

Q When do these groups form and are there differences in the way they behave?

It's fascinating to find that as early as 3 or 4, boys and girls not only choose different toys and playmates but the patterns of interaction within the groups are different too.

Maccoby and Martin (1990) described the girls' pattern as an enabling style, which included requests, and making supportive suggestions, i.e. tactics to keep the interaction going. Boys, on the other hand, used a restrictive style. This came from observing boys trying to outwit their peers, cutting down their suggestions, e.g. 'That's sad, we're not playing that', and generally being boastful and competitive. This may explain why some children find it so difficult to sustain their participation in play activities. They may be hurt by comments that were really part of the group culture rather than being personal, but they still cause the sensitive child to withdraw.

PLAYING WITH TOYS

Q Some children have favourite toys and will not be parted from them. Why's that? Does this show insecurity?

A great deal can be gleaned from observing the way children play with toys. It is very revealing is to see whether the toys are given a personality or are just used as familiar objects, i.e. as comforters. Often children choose the same toy, e.g. a boy choosing a truck with wheels that spin, but gradually this diminishes as the play develops. For example, the truck might become part of a game of making roads in the sand, and then possibly the game could include another truck-interested child who would build dams, or the children would include figures working or travelling on the trucks.

But another child might repeat the same action, e.g. whirling the wheels close to his ear, over and over again and resist involving anyone else. This is static play and if it endures could be the sign that obsessions are limiting the child's play.

Q What about if the toy is a cuddly one, for example, a teddy or a toy dog?

Again, observe to see if the child gives the toy a personality. Does it have a name and does the child care for it, e.g. wrap it in a blanket and sing to it? Or is it just there, a toy with no personality, no soul?

Q What would this mean?

Well, if this behaviour occurred with other difficulties, e.g. avoiding eye contact or not interacting sensitively with other children, then the child may have communication difficulties, for example in the way that children on the autistic spectrum do. But this needs very careful assessment before any such suggestion is made. Is the child unused to playing with others and using the toy as a shield? Has the child been ill and needs to hold the toy to show he is busy while he looks out to see what other children are doing?

MAKING A FRIEND: DEVELOPING ALTRUISM AND EMPATHY

Q One of the most difficult things to watch is a child who doesn't get to play. Nurseries often put notices up saying 'We are all friends here', but often there's a child who can't seem to make a friend. How can we help?

Most parents' immediate hope when their children go to nursery or school is that the child will find a friend. And indeed, if they find a staunch one, then there are likely to be fewer traumas in growing up. But when this doesn't happen, children can be left out – is there anything more heartbreaking than the question, 'Why will nobody let me play?'. Sometimes, of course, the answer may be obvious, because the child is aggressive or pushy or even unkempt, but often even experienced staff can think of no reason why. So looking into the stages of developing friendships can be a first step in providing an answer.

WHEN DOES IT ALL BEGIN?

When 3-year-olds are asked, 'Who is your friend?', they will smile and offer names that may vary from day to day. But the question, 'Why do you like him?' is likely to be shrugged off or answered 'He's big' or 'I don't know'. The 'bigness' is a criterion that is beginning to permeate the child's thinking as being a desirable state, for he will have heard adults comment in admiring voices, 'Isn't he big?', but it will not mean 'big' as in offering protection or have more subtle underpinnings at this stage. The qualities very young children mention are superficial ones similar to those they use to describe themselves. It's a 'what you see is what you get' time.

But at 4 or 5 children usually have a much more enduring and comprehensive list of criteria: 'He plays with me on the bikes', 'He looks out for me and sticks up for me'. Appearance is beginning to be less important than personal qualities such as loyalty and skill even though the children may lack the language to describe what they feel.

69

Looking out for one another is the beginning of the development of altruism, i.e. caring for someone else even at some cost to oneself, and empathy, i.e. recognising and being sympathetic to others' feelings. This develops at about 2 or 3, i.e. at the time children begin to play with others. When children offer a toy or welcome a needy child into a game, they are showing signs that these qualities are developing. When they play, they increasingly recognise the emotions of others and respond in supportive or sympathetic ways. Often this is done by reading non-verbal cues, e.g. recognising that the child who sits with bowed shoulders and hidden eyes is anxious or sad.

DEVELOPING ALTRUISM AND EMPATHY

Eisenberg (1992) shows how important developing altruism and empathy is, for children who show more altruistic behaviour are the ones who regulate their own emotions well. They show more positive, and fewer negative, emotions when encountering new situations and are more willing to try new things. But some children can show too much altruism and overwhelm their peers. Older children have been known to steal things to pass to another child in the hope of earning friendship. This may *appear* to work, but the donor is likely to be rejected when he is found out or when the supplies fail to be delivered. So how can children like this be helped to find a friend?

Bee (2004) argues that it is the activity children *enjoy* that is the key, rather than the personality of the different children. Discovering this and pairing children so that they can discuss favourite hobbies or games is one suggestion that seems to work. Another is to discuss with the isolated children how they might get into a game. One boy waited till there was a noisy playground game and then joined in the cacophony, running and screaming as he went. He was in!

But early pro-social behaviour can change. Comforting another child, a lovely sight in the earliest years, seems to diminish in 6–10-year-olds. Younger children, even younger disadvantaged children, will donate more to others described as needy than those in older groups. Is this because they are altruistic and find pleasure in giving? Are they not so materialistic as those children with more toys and clothes, or do they not realise that giving things away means they have less? But generalities, of course, are only a part of the picture. It is interesting to note, however, that family-rearing practices can be overridden by the intrinsic intuitions of feelings developed by nature rather than nurture. The studies of adopted children show that altruistic practices tend to match the first home background better than the adopted one, even when the child has been adopted as a baby.

Q But what about children who just won't conform? They can disrupt the whole nursery. They defy all the staff and are quite likely to hurt the other children?

This is when some physical restraint is justified in my view. Severe aggression may well be 'inherited' to some degree, and is also linked to irritable and aggressive parenting behaviour. Children may have witnessed aggressive ways of solving disputes at home and have not had guidance in using other ways. Findings like this have led to classes in child management skills.

Generally unprovoked aggression makes children unpopular, yet these rejected children try aggression to solve their difficulties, possibly because they know no other way. On the other hand, out-of-control children may have a neurological difference such as ADHD. Their neurotransmitters are providing them with too much stimulation and they are driven to run, jump and shout, even when they know that this is not the way to behave. Many earnestly try to change, but don't know how.

GROWING UP WITH SIBLINGS: THE IMPACT ON EMOTIONAL DEVELOPMENT

Q Is it important where children come in the family? I've often heard that the middle one of three has a hard time.

Most children grow up with siblings and in the pre-school years these relationships are particularly important. Earlier research concentrated on birth order and studied the aspirations and outcomes of the first, second and third child. They found that first-borns tended to be more goal-oriented and anxious, while later children were more sociable, and more easily swayed by the opinions of others. But this was quite simplistic, because many variables, such as family income and even the sex of the other children, were complicating the picture. Newer research asks more complex questions, e.g. do parents interact differently with siblings and how does this influence the relationships they build with each other? In a longitudinal study (Bee 2002), researchers found that older siblings often began by imitating their new brother or sister, crying lustily or wanting a bottle of milk, but by the time the baby was a year old this stopped. Thereafter, the younger one copied the elder. They might show both aggression and helpful behaviours to each other. The siblings hit one another and snatched their toys, but gradually ambivalence developed as each child concentrated on their own development.

Do parents treat siblings differently? While most would deny any favouritism, the children's perceptions of this can be the basis of feelings of inadequacy and/or being second best. 'Just because my brother's in a wheelchair, we have to do everything he wants', muttered one frustrated child who obviously felt guilty at having such thoughts. But even when there are no extreme situations like that, parents can show what other children construe as favouritism, although they may deny such a charge.

CASE STUDY

Jake was a sensitive, gentle boy. His sister Grace was a tomboy, always in scrapes. Now although her mother appeared to admonish her, the tone she used, 'What a rascal you are', was complimentary, making Jake feel he was inadequate. He wished he could be a tomboy too. Over a period of time the resentment built up, and, especially when copying his sister, he in turn behaved badly. That was different. His act was seen to be malicious rather than naughty, and there were no hardly hidden smiles to soften the blow. No one recognised that Jake was trying to find ways to be on a par with his sister. He became an unhappy, withdrawn little boy.

So subtleties in child-rearing practices abound and the children soon learn to evaluate them. These can affect their emotional state, either building or knocking their confidence. Many children try to change, as the picture they have of themselves doesn't please them – but most often they don't know how. It is when frustration boils over that adults see the results of poor child-rearing skills.

ETHNIC AWARENESS, IDENTITY AND PREJUDICE

Ethnic awareness

Q I remember having a little African girl in my nursery. All the other children were fair skinned and wouldn't have met a child from Africa before, yet they gave no sign of noticing any difference? When does this develop?

As children grow they become aware of differences in hair and skin colour and in facial appearance and body-build, i.e. differences due to ethnic origin. By age 4 or 5 children will recognise basic distinctions and by age 8 or 9 they realise that these are permanent, despite superficial changes in attire.

Ethnic identity

This is awareness of one's own ethnicity. It is usually assessed by asking children to look at pictures of dolls and to point out which one is like them. However, a child might be swayed by a kind facial expression or a preference for the clothes the dolls wear, so it is important to test this using several dolls and/or on different occasions. Children need to know *who* they are and to be proud of belonging to their cultural heritage. In 2006 children from impoverished parts of Namibia are being taken to other regions to appreciate the scenery and the wildlife and so develop national pride. Experiences like this help them to appreciate their culture and their country. Nurseries here are trying to follow this by embracing different cultural practices and demonstrating to all children that differences enrich lives.

Ethnic prejudice

Q When does prejudice begin?

It can be difficult to separate out ethnic preference from prejudice unless it is an overt act. Children at 4 may prefer to play with their own ethnic group without attributing any negative overtones to those in the other group. In cases of preference, when children from different ethnic backgrounds do play together, there would be no change in their behaviour. On the other hand, prejudice implies a negative evaluation of another person on the basis of sex, disability or race. Largely absent at age 3 and 4, this develops at age 5 or 6, when children begin to see others as being different and they tend to link negative assessments with this. In his film *Child of Our Time*, Robert Winston showed young children from a minority group pointing out pictures of people they would like to play with. In the main, these were children in the majority group. This was so sad, and shows how much work is still to be done.

Q What do nurseries do to combat this?

Most practitioners now try to understand the backgrounds and religions of all the children in their care and they celebrate the important festivals and special days of all the groups so that the children's learning is extended in positive ways. Divali has a place in the curriculum just like Christmas and the Chinese New Year, and the children share all the exciting, very different things. Parents come into the nursery to bake traditional dishes with the children, and they show traditional costumes, e.g. kilts and saris, or share making artefacts such as Chinese lanterns or dragons. Working together in groups like this can improve inter-racial respect.

This cultural richness is very important. Children have only one childhood, and early years staff must try to make sense of all the complex understandings and relationships that make children what they are. Practitioners are often nervous of being seen to favour one child and can only be vigilant about treating *each* child with respect and giving *each one* a fair share of teaching and listening time. This is not an easy thing to do.

■ **FIGURE 4.3**
Making bagpipes
adds to the fun in
celebrating Burns'
Night

Chapter 5

Understanding moral development

As children mature and become more independent, they are expected to make moral judgements about what is right and what is wrong. This usually involves them in following the prevailing, accepted, cultural 'rules' of right and wrong. Often these are internalised, the children observing their parents rather than having explicit explanations of these rules. And some groups will live by different rules to others. Surely we all need rules if society is not to be chaotic? But when children act according to these rules, are they making moral judgements or are they only following a code that will ensure they are praised or rewarded for so doing? Can we/should we/how should we teach children to be 'good'? Is there a fine line between co-operation, conformity and coercion?

Play is the focus of the early years curriculum. It is a child's world, a time when children develop understandings and learn the skills they need to cope as they become more independent. Surely then, adults should be helping children learn appropriate behaviour as they play? There have been many authors who have resisted adults' attempts to do just that, considering intervention morally reprehensible. Cohen (1990) was one such. He was adamant that adults should not intervene in children's play. 'How can we, long out of practice oldies teach children how to play?' he asked. He continued: 'and when I hear of adults saying things like "at play the children should learn to take turns and share things," I have to ask, "Are there social engineers on the swings?".' He considered that any intervention removed both freedom and ownership from the children. 'Some children,' he explained, 'mistakenly thinking adults know better, will acquiesce, but then they wait for adults to tell them what to do.' He claims that such intervention denies children the opportunity to be creative and imaginative. 'Some will rebel,' he adds. 'I hope they do!'

As a dancer many years ago, I was taught that I had to learn the movement technique first, and only when these skills were learned could I use them to be expressive. The technique was the foundation that guaranteed safety (from injury) and survival (employment). So dances that were known to 'be good' were taught until the technique was mastered. But then another teacher explained, 'From the start, all technique should be expressive, so that you can be creative and make the dance your own.' The trouble was that many of the dancers, unused to such freedom, could not use it. They had not developed the creative side of their thinking when they were mastering the technique. Creativity didn't happen as a natural follow-on after all. Of course, no one had explained this progression, i.e. that this was what was supposed to happen, either. Does this analogy match teaching in the early years? Is there a way to pass on the techniques without stultifying imagination? Will this make intervening in children's play 'right?'

Q So, in the early years, how do children develop a sense of what is right or wrong? Where do they get this information?

Perhaps in a chapter on morality, it is best to answer by posing more questions. For example, are the many instances of things 'one just doesn't do' explained to children, or are these constraints context-bound? They learn that it's 'naughty' to barge around the nursery shouting and letting off steam, but in the park, that's perfectly all right. And when a child tells another 'you're fat'– when the child is fat – is that wrong? Hurtful statements are not socially acceptable, but adults can worry in private about a child's obesity, keeping the concern from the child; or they may consider the weight is puppy fat and it will disappear in its own time. But they may be denying the child the chance to do something about it. Who is 'right'?

Most children are expected to absorb this moral sense from the role-models around them, and, of course, these people may have a very different code from the one(s) taught in schools. Some parents may scorn people who work. Some regard nursery and school as free childminding, not education at all, while others want to push their young children into inappropriate formal learning. Another group is happy to leave education to the staff, either because of a laissez-faire attitude or because they genuinely believe that the staff are professionals who know best. These different stances are absorbed by the children and must affect their perceptions of what is right and wrong and, particularly for older children, how they value their time in school. In turn this affects their behaviour.

Some parents may have given a great deal of thought to the moral well-being of their children, but at times of stress, fatigue and even love, may understandably lack the time or energy they need to stand by their principles. So the children receive mixed messages. And if the parents disagree on what their child should be allowed to do and say, what then? The children soon learn to play one off against the other. But is this only the parents' dilemma? How often have we asked children in the nursery to do as we say rather than copy what we do?

Other parents believe that any repression will mar a child's free spirit and that their children will successfully make their own moral code for themselves. They believe that total freedom of choice is essential before children can be said to be making moral judgements. The different groups are passing on very different lifestyle messages to their children. Furthermore, these children, in another setting, may be judged for following the way things are done or not done at home.

Q How do children learn to make judgements about what is right and wrong?

This is a huge topic. The most reported researchers in this area are Kohlberg (1969) and Piaget (1932). Piaget claimed that, in their early years, children were bound by concrete findings, i.e. what they could see and hear. They were not attuned to abstract competences such as recognising intention. So he devised an experiment to test this theory. His experiment aimed to show whether children took intention into account when making judgements about right or wrong and when giving punishment for an act. When would children see intention as a contributory factor to the outcome and so affect their judgement of what was done? Piaget told a group of children two short stories, then asked them their thoughts.

Story 1
A little boy called John was in his room when he was called down to dinner. He went into the kitchen where the meal was to be, but behind the door was a tray with 15 cups. John didn't know that the cups were there, but when he knocked them over, they all broke.

Story 2

One day when his Mum was out, a little boy called Henry climbed up on a chair to get some jam from a cupboard. He couldn't reach it, but as he stretched up, he slipped and broke a cup that was on the shelf.

The children were asked 'which child was the naughtiest?'. Do you think it was John or was it Henry?

The 5-year-olds found that 'both children were naughty' but when it came to the question of punishment, then the boy that broke 15 cups was thought to deserve 'more slaps' (Jack aged 5). They were only concerned by the outcome, i.e. the amount of damage, and did not consider the intention, i.e. that John could not have known the cups were there and so could not have prevented the accident. Teegan, aged 7, however, claimed that Henry 'knew he was doing wrong – he did it on purpose and he should be smacked'. In contrast, 'John had an accident,' she explained. 'He didn't know the cups were there.' 'Who put them in that silly place?' asked Gail, aged 9. She had a much more sophisticated conception of events and was anxious to follow the story to a logical conclusion by finding the real culprit.

In line with Piaget's work on conservation, later researchers claimed that explanations or more child-friendly language could help children to develop awareness of intention at an earlier age. However, Piaget was looking for implicit understandings, i.e. what children *brought* to a situation, not what they could do after teaching. So responses depend at least to some extent on how children are brought up, e.g. whether they are taught to consider scenarios as problem-solving events and whether they are ever encouraged to justify their thoughts and actions.

Q When we talk about how children should be brought up, we probably think back to our own experiences and try to extract the good parts and avoid the mistakes (in our retrospective view) our own families made. But each of us has only one life experience and that may be very different from the one another person has. How are we to know what else goes on, and what the implications are for children brought up with different sets of standards?

Styles of parenting *are* very different. Let's look at the work of Maccoby and Martin (1990) who describe four types.

AUTHORITARIAN PARENTS

Authoritarian parents insist on high levels of control, but show little warmth or responsiveness to their children. They are there to be seen and not heard. Children from these families are used to being told what to do with little room for manoeuvre. They hear the instruction 'do this' or 'don't do that' with no explanation as to why and no leeway allowed. The parents may consider that strict discipline encourages high standards. So, in the early years setting, in a less restrictive atmosphere where commands are replaced by requests, children may be confused and unable to make decisions or imagine the implications of their actions. On the other hand, they may revel in the freedom and become loud, aggressive and out of control. Parents who smack to get obedience are most often in this authoritarian group.

PERMISSIVE PARENTS

The permissive style is high in nurturing, but low in maturity demands, control and communication. Children brought up in this way can enjoy a great deal of freedom, but lack guidance and do not know how to behave appropriately in different settings when they can't do as they please. Indulgent or over-permissive parents may find that their children show signs of aggression too. These can surface when the children have to do as they are told. The children are less likely to want to take responsibility and may do less well in school.

AUTHORITATIVE PARENTS

This pattern has been shown to produce the most reliable, self-confident children. The parents are in control and respond to the children's needs so that they feel secure, yet the children know they can ask questions and receive considered explanations. Dowling (2004) explains that such loving support 'helps the "right" behaviour to stem from a basis of understanding', and she claims 'children in this kind of relationship with their parents, will want to behave in a way that pleases them'. But perhaps this fluctuates as other people, e.g. the peer group, replace the parents and the teachers as the most 'significant others' in children's lives?

NEGLECTING PARENTS

Children who are subject to this pattern are most likely to be aggressive and hostile. This can be down to the psychological unavailability of the parents. They may be depressed or ill or bored by the difficulties of bringing up children and 'escape' mentally or even physically. The children in turn are likely to show great difficulties in forming relationships and, when older, they are likely to attach to antisocial groups made up of other neglected or rejected children, who may be the only ones who empathise with this kind of behaviour.

MORAL REASONING AND MORAL BEHAVIOUR

Q So how can early years practitioners come to understand the intricacies of moral development when the children in their care have come from a myriad of family and community backgrounds?

There are two aspects of moral development that are interdependent, but the complexity comes in that one does not always follow the other.

The first is *moral reasoning*, i.e. how we judge whether an action is right or wrong; the second is *moral behaviour*, which doesn't always follow. The first is about knowing, and the second, doing. For example, a child may *know* it's wrong to steal someone else's sweets, but the temptation can be too strong and the deed is done anyway. Whether feelings of guilt follow or whether the child justifies (to themself) their action, e.g. 'Well, I am never allowed sweets and he has them all the time', depends on their stage of moral reasoning and the influence of their home environment. If the child has been brought up to take what they want, then their perspective on what they have done will be different to that of a child who knows their parents will not approve – but that child may take the sweets nonetheless. On the other hand, the second child may act correctly and deny themself the treat, but feel frustrated by being constrained by their conscience.

The reactions of parents can be hugely different too, as the following extreme examples will show. Smith, Blades and Cowie (2002) cite the examples of two sets of parents whose children were killed by other children. The first was the toddler Jamie Bulger, killed in the UK by two 10-year-olds, and the second was a 6-year-old child, Silje, in Norway. The public described Jamie's killers as 'evil' and the outcry made it clear that long prison sentences should be the punishment. But in Norway Silje's mother found she could not hate the three young boys who did the dreadful deed. This was 'because they were children'. These very different responses reflect very different thoughts on when children should be held morally responsible for their actions. Would the forgiving response help the parents cope and allow them to move forward? Was this better (for them), than the fear that engulfed parents in the UK and led to some playgrounds being encased in wire fences and children at home 'not being allowed out to play'? There are no easy answers to questions like this, except that moral judgements must be made in the context of the family and community to which the child belongs.

When do these dilemmas begin? If children come from a poverty-stricken home with no moral guidance, should they be expected to behave and be treated differently?

CASE STUDY

Carly tells of her experience:

> Well, we had tried just about everything to make Josh behave. He's a bright boy who seeks attention all the time. The trouble was that the other children knew he was the naughty one and they goaded him to misbehave and enjoyed him getting scolded. He didn't seem to mind; in fact he just shrugged and looked as if he was enjoying the attention, so scolding didn't do any good. We were advised to note how often his name was called out and do it less, so we tried that; we even tried to ignore bad behaviour that didn't hurt any of the other children, but that had little effect as well. So the next move was to give him responsibility and let him know he was important. 'Josh, we have chosen you to check that the story sacks have all the books and toys,' we said. Immediately there was an outcry. 'I wanted to do that and I've been good all day,' cried Alana, 'why does he get to do it when he's a bad boy?'

How can staff explain to children that the punishment doesn't always fit the crime? Will any of these techniques work when children are so young? At what age can *any* child be thought to be morally responsible? These are difficult questions. Thankfully, even in severely disadvantaged homes where the children have had to learn survival skills and become streetwise early, most children will not harm others, at least not severely. But many have to have repeated explanations of what is acceptable behaviour and some have to be restrained, even excluded, if their behaviour threatens others. And even at this early age, some children bully others,

81

DISCUSSION TOPIC

Kay is a medical student and during her holiday she went to a shelter for children with HIV in Africa. In material terms these children had nothing, yet they could enjoy a game with one burst ball, kicking it happily in the sand. All the children played; there was no 'choosing teams' and leaving one child last. These children just joined in without worrying about being picked; there were no rules and when goals were scored between two canes stuck into the sand, everyone clapped.

When Kay said to one little boy, 'what a nice T-shirt you are wearing,' his immediate response was to try to take it off. 'You must have it, for I love you,' was his response. This was the only T-shirt he had.

Kay explained how humble she felt, and she became determined to raise funds to send toys to the children. But would these toys introduce the idea that material things were more important? Would all the children still smile?

What is the best way forward?

and steal or spoil their work, apparently without thought, even appearing to gain pleasure by their malicious acts. Yet others, no matter what their apparent disadvantages, are very caring and share what little they have with no thought for themselves.

If children are to develop moral reasoning for themselves and gradually build a value base, they must be able to think through various courses of action and make decisions about what to do and how to do it. They must be able to anticipate the consequences of their behaviour. How much harder must that be if the children have not had any consistent reactions to the behaviour at home.

Q How does the age of children influence what they do?

From his research into how children came to resolve moral dilemmas, Piaget (1932) distinguished three age-related stages. He claimed that up to age 4 or 5, the rules of a game or rules at play were not understood; in the second stage the rules were seen as coming from a higher authority (God, adults, teachers) and could not be changed. The third stage at 9 or 10 years saw the children negotiating rules and changing them if everyone in the group agreed.

Piaget's stages have been criticised (the language in some tests was not child-friendly but once that had been changed the children achieved more at an earlier age; and other researchers replicating the tests have similarly found that with explanations children could show achievement at earlier ages), but he was the first to set a stage or maturational theory – he was not talking about how children reacted to teaching, and children long ago had very different upbringings to those they have now (my thoughts). Despite these criticisms his work has stayed as of immense importance for parents and teachers learning about how children develop.

So, at age 4 or 5, children may learn rules about behaviour in an instrumental way; they may accept them, rather like learning by rote, without realising or asking 'why?'. They may pull away in frustration when they are thwarted, yet not able to offer an acceptable alternative. They may have several sets of rules for different settings and obey or reject them on different days. Only when they reach the age of being able to weigh up implications and act accordingly can they be said to make moral judgements on their own.

Q This would seem to suggest that it doesn't matter what children do? Surely this can't be right?

Of course it's not! This is the time when the children absorb values and learn about co-operation and sharing and trusting. At this critical time, when the children are learning faster than at any other time, role-models can help them understand morally sound ways that, we hope, will stand them in good stead in the future, no matter what slings and arrows they meet.

Two traumatic events are separation of the parents and the death of a close relative or a much-loved pet. How can staff support young children when these unhappy events intrude in their young lives, before they can foresee the implications of each, and when their parents are also distraught?

Q It must be terrible for children when their parents separate? What kind of reactions should we expect?

Any conflict between parents can be very distressing for children who then have divided loyalties. When this is the norm, anxieties pervade their childhood and translate into their having more difficulty in sustaining

KEY TOPIC

Key topic: understand-ing young children when their parents separate or divorce

friendships and focusing on their work in school (Katz and Gottman 1993). And when disagreements and arguments lead to separation, this is not usually an immediate decision. Unhappiness and anxiety will have begun long before that time. Awareness of the effects of warring parents on their children needs to be recognised well before separation or divorce occurs.

When separation does happen, Davies and Cummings (1994) found that in their research group (made up of children of age 4 and 5), these same children were still traumatised at 9 years old. Their teachers reported them as showing much more antisocial behaviour than occurred in groups of other children of the same age and of similar social status. So effects of separation on children can be profound and long-lasting.

The effects have been found to vary according to the ages of the affected children, with the youngest groups less affected because they are less aware of the implications that accompany divorce. They may not realise that such a decision will not be revoked, thinking that the absent parent will come home at a later date. When this doesn't happen, they may decide that they have caused the split and be consumed by guilt. Although irrational, this is nonetheless very painful for the child, especially if the child cannot confide in or be reassured by the parent who is still there.

The material deficits resulting from divorce are likely to cause hardship too. Moving home may be necessary and, for the first time, money may be short and a topic of wrangling between parents. A non-working parent may have to get a job and the split may mean that one set of grandparents, who might have helped out with childminding or even financially, lose contact or feel alienated, causing more grief all round. In the extreme, children may be abused if they are thought to have caused the disharmony. This can happen if parents conceive of relationships in terms of power struggles so that they are constantly tense. Studies show that children with step-parents may be abused too. Why should this be? It could be that it is not in a step-parent's genetic make up to invest in children who are not related. While most step-parents make huge efforts to be accepted and are often successful, some of the strategies they try are not able to work because the new members of the family are seen (by the children and possibly the grandparents) as intruders, even as the cause of a close relation being ousted from the family group.

It is not easy to see how the early years setting can help, beyond giving the children time to talk and reassuring them that the early years setting will stay the same. Of course, allowances have to be made, but practitioners are often at a loss what to say. What advice is given? How can the effects be minimalised and the consequences reduced? Several pieces of advice for parents, carers and teachers taken from different research reports are listed below. They are:

- Keep the children in the same environment; keep changes to routine to a minimum, and provide familiar activities and experiences to give the children security.
- Parents who retain the main role are advised to try to maintain a quality of life for themselves, e.g. to continue with activities that were enjoyed before the separation. Keeping up a wide circle of friendships has positive results; one very important result being that the children don't become isolated.
- Practitioners are advised to *listen* to the child, but not to take sides. They have to remember that the child may be biased by not appreciating all the ins and outs of the situation. Moreover, if the practitioner blames a parent, the children are likely to want to defend him or her, regardless of where they themselves might allocate blame. Practitioners are urged to stay in contact with the remaining parent, staying positive and not breaching the child's confidence. Any suspicion that this has occurred will destroy any trust in the relationship, which at this stage might at least partially compensate for the one lost at home.

Many of these strategies depend on getting to know the individual children and family as well as the community context in which they are placed. The nursery is the place to start building relationships, and staff there should be given the time to get to grips with these complex issues, for separation and/or divorce impact on nearly every child, either directly or as a friend.

COPING WITH BEREAVEMENT

Q How do practitioners in the early years support children who are experiencing bereavement?

Again, it's a question of understanding each family's perspective, gauging how much the child wants to know, and finding what the children are likely to ask (from the literature or experienced teachers).

85

Q What do children think when a friend or a pet dies?

Adults know that death is irreversible, that it comes to everyone, and that families are usually very sad. Young children have a different set of beliefs. Bee (2002) explains: 'Pre-school children believe that death can be reversed, through magic or prayer or wishful thinking' or even, perhaps, like the princess in the story book, by a kiss from a prince. They also believe that the members of their own family can avoid death.

Many believe that 'children can't die – you have to be really old and ill'. This can stand children with terminal or life-threatening illnesses in good stead. 'If I take my medicine, I'll go back to school next term,' explained one 5-year-old who was slowly losing the battle with cancer.

Understanding this stance, i.e. don't burden the children with more detail than they request, will inhibit lengthy explanations that may only serve to confuse the children. It will be vital to discuss with the family how they want the nursery staff to talk with the child. Some disparate views show the controversy here. 'Don't mention Granny dying at all,' said one Mum, 'for when he's at nursery I want him to be able to forget all the sadness that's at home.' 'I think how you dealt with the hamster dying, burying it and making a special song and having a little ceremony, helped Charlie understand,' said another Mum. 'She learned it was OK to be sad and that it was good to keep talking; she knew she could ask questions but it was awful when she asked where the hamster had gone and when it would come back. I wished we were religious because that would give us some comfort' (Collins 2005).

Different cultures regard death quite differently. In some North American cultures, children learn that death is a time for composure and dignity. It is talked of as 'part of nature's natural cycle' and as such it is not feared. In Mexico, death is celebrated, even having a 'Day for the Dead' in the midst of their festivals.

In the UK today there is much more talk of celebrating the person's life than mourning those who have died. But, of course, it may take time for the reality and the rhetoric to blend. Meantime, in the nursery, practitioners have to listen to and support the child, and often this extends to the adult members of the families as well.

Chapter 6

Understanding intellectual development

While most professionals and parents value all aspects of their children's development and come to understand how the interplay of each contributes to learning, many tend to see the social, emotional, moral and motor contributions as underpinnings of the intellectual one. This may well depend on what they see as the purpose of education in nurseries and schools. They may have an instrumental view of education and see its purpose as providing the children with the skills to get a job that, in turn, allows them to achieve a good standard of living, in which case they are

■ **FIGURE 6.1**
Learning can be
a multi-sensory
experience

87 ■

■ **FIGURE 6.2** Singing and playing percussion helps rhythm and timing as well as providing lots of fun

likely to view mathematics and literacy skills as the most important. On the other hand, some may take a broader view and want their children to be creative and imaginative, enabling them to appreciate the 'good things' around them. This is an expressive or aesthetic stance. They will be anxious that music, drama, art and movement are given prime time.

But of course, the two ways of thinking are not mutually exclusive. Professionals in the early years, appreciating the intellectual learning potential in both these stances, strive to provide a balance that includes all the topics in a play-based curriculum.

Once again practitioners were asked taxing questions.

Q When you focus on intellectual development, what are the skills and competences that you want your children to be able to know or do?

- Basic counting (i.e. numbers 1–5). For example, the number of children at the water tray; the number of buns in a baker's shop.
- Know their colours – at least the primary ones. The 4-year-olds learn about mixing colours and how they change to make

others. They learn more subtle shades, e.g. lilac, at appropriate times (for example, when the tree blossoms).

- Make circles and patterns (i.e. emergent writing). For example, some children will want to write their name, while others will want to learn to control a pencil or paintbrush.
- Listen to a story and remember/anticipate the sequence (for example, in 'The Three Little Pigs').
- Clap out the rhythm of jingles and nursery rhymes.
- Be able to follow a routine and to become more independent. To remember things without always having to ask.
- Stay focused on a task for some time (for example, arrange beads in sizes or colours then thread them). The children need to be aware of the pattern they are creating.
- Show respect for other cultures (for example, festivals, foods, ways of dressing) and for other children.
- Know how to look after the environment (for example, through helping in the garden and appreciating the activities of the wildlife). Indoors, realise that tidying and recycling are important.
- Understand the foods children should choose to keep themselves healthy. Enjoy them at snack time.
- Recognise their names and the sounds of a few individual letters such as 's' and 't'.
- Be able to remember a message for their parents.
- Know who is fetching them and get ready independently.
- Be able to role-play in the different areas, for example, be a nurse in the hospital corner or a fire-engine driver.

These descriptions of what the children should know or be able to do over the two years in nursery do sound as if the content of the curriculum is decided in advance and is taught according to a set of predetermined criteria. But while these targets certainly *guide* planning, again *balance* comes into play. This time it is a balance between pre-set curricular goals (the timing of the introduction of those goals and the children's readiness to absorb and interact with materials and experiences) and allowing the children to make decisions about the topic they wish to study. And, as children develop at different rates and learn best in different ways, as well as come to nursery from widely differing backgrounds, decisions about when and how to introduce new learning are part of the discussions the team will hold every day. To be totally appropriate for this age group of children, the nursery curriculum has to be based on developing learning through play.

Q So there are a number of questions to be answered before we make plans?

Important questions would be:

- What do children coming to nursery already know?
- What skills are already developing?
- What learning experiences will allow children to fulfil their potential while achieving the competences or targets in the guidelines/curriculum documentation?

When children come to nursery they have already learned a great deal. Although at birth the nervous system is not well developed, babies learn quickly. In fact, some would say that the first year is the fastest learning time of all. Babies are curious and they are motivated to learn and to go on learning; these inbuilt attributes lead to experiences that develop connections between the neural pathways in the brain. These encourage them to learn some more – we are powerless to prevent it. As long ago as 1974, Trevarthen made a number of claims that still provide nursery personnel with ammunition to stress the importance of the work they do. He wrote:

Children learn 50 per cent of everything they know in the first five years.

The brain of every child in every culture goes through the same developmental stages.

Curiosity is needed to develop the brain.

Children must have the right experiences at the right time.

No nursery practitioner would be surprised at the first of these claims, and indeed much of the exhilaration in teaching in the nursery setting comes from observing how fast most children learn new things. They surprise and delight by their swift progress, even on occasion telling practitioners things they do not know. They devise their own descriptive words to communicate and provide the source of many chortles as they do. One child asked what was the best thing in the nursery solemnly replied, 'Buggery'. Well, they had studied a wormery and an antery. How else would one describe the study of 'minibeasts' in the garden?

The second claim offers some consolation for planners and observers. It means that learning experiences that suit a 3-year-old from one country should be appropriate for a child from another and the children should respond in much same way. Of course, there will be enrichment in sharing ideas that are culture-specific, but basic activities such as those found in each area, e.g. water play, picture puzzles, using the soft play area, or small world resources, can enhance the learning of all children.

The third claims that in most young children motivation to learn is high. This is intrinsic and explains why most nursery children can't wait to begin. But to fulfil Trevarthen's fourth claim practitioners also have to consider the timing and pacing of introducing new learning to ensure that the children are not overwhelmed and confused. This could happen more easily for children learning English as their second language.

LEARNING LANGUAGE

Learning language is a good example of Trevarthen's fourth claim (the one about critical learning times, i.e. when children learn certain things most easily). At 6 months babies can discriminate all the sound contrasts that appear in any language, including sounds they do not hear in the language spoken to them each day, but by 10 months this is starting to disappear. This was the same for Hindi babies, Japanese babies and English babies. So early immersion in a different language is the best timing. Bee (2002) advises that in households where parents have different native tongues, each should speak only their own to the child. In this way the child will be bilingual with no confusion.

KEY TOPIC

Learning language

Q **The early ability to discriminate sounds, then, must be well ahead of the children's ability to make them?**

That's true. Babies sing the tune before they speak the words. Their understanding is well ahead of their ability to respond with words. This is often true for children with additional learning needs as well, so practitioners need to recognise this and not delay input till the children can respond verbally.

91

Q What are the early signs of developing language?

As early as 1 or 2 months babies gurgle and make cooing sounds. Some-times they can be heard trying these sounds at different levels and pitches and chortling with pleasure as they do. Between 9 and 12 months this develops into monosyllabic babbling – repetition of the same syllable, e.g. 'dadadada' or 'mamamama'. Naturally, parents are charmed by this early form of communication, which is really practice for the next stage, 'jargon' (often called variegated babbling). In jargon, babies string together different syllables with intonations that *sound* like sentences. Often adults repeat these back to the baby as a game and this is this basis of turn-taking in language development. If turn-taking is difficult for 3-year-olds, playing games like peek-a-boo can instil the 'speak then wait and listen' idea.

Non-verbal communication

Of course, children don't depend on vocals to make their needs known. Non-verbal communication conveys most – some would claim 90 per cent – of the meaning in a message. Think of the baby stretching out towards a favourite toy. The actions of clasping and unclasping a hand and possibly grizzling as an accompaniment, leave no doubt as to the child's wish. So babies can communicate their wishes long before they can talk.

Understanding language

Q But when do babies really understand the words that they hear?

Receptive language, which is the name given to the understanding that precedes the expressive language stage, begins at about 9 or 10 months, and by 12 months the babies should understand about 30 words. By 13 months, though, the understanding rises to about 130 words – a large increase. So although they do not speak, babies are learning all about the sounds and the intonations of their language and they benefit from being exposed to a rich variety of words.

Emergence of the first words

First words generally appear at about 12–13 months. These may be made-up words rather than recognised words. Until about 18 months these are single words. Toddlers often combine a word with a gesture to clarifying what they mean. They might point to a pair of shoes and say only 'Daddy's' when they mean 'There are Daddy's shoes'. This shows that their comprehension is much more developed than their articulation.

It is so interesting to find that deaf babies of deaf parents go through the same first stages in their language development at the same rate. At about 12 months they will make a sign, e.g. raising an imaginary cup to their lips to indicate they are thirsty. And hearing children of deaf parents still speak at the same time as if they had been born into families without disability. Yet they have probably been exposed to much less verbal interaction.

When the language spurt occurs at around 18 months, most of the words children volunteer are 'naming words', e.g. 'doggie', 'car', 'hat' and so on. A smaller number use an expressive style. Their earliest sentences are linked to social relationships using prepositions, 'I want Mum' rather than naming objects. The expressive style sounds more advanced than the naming or referential style but they are really only different ways of thinking. This reminds observers to look for individual differences when they identify developmental norms.

Q From what you've said, it would be important to read stories to babies, even when the words seem rather hard?

'Reading together' is important from the earliest days because the children are learning that the words on the page are the sounds that are heard. At 9 months or so the baby can begin pointing to objects and naming them or querying what they are called. More expressive babies will want you to explain, 'This is the little girl's doll', i.e. explaining social relationships rather than building a vocabulary of nouns.

Q I've heard of 'Motherese'. What's that?

'Motherese' or, as it is now called, 'infant-directed language', is the simply constructed repetitive language mothers use to communicate with their babies. Parents tend to speak to their babies using a higher pitch and this appears to intrigue the baby and keep it listening. So simple sentences are internalised through repetition and imitation.

Talking in sentences

By 30 months infants have a vocabulary of about 600 words and by 5 years children have 15,000 words, an increase of 15 new words a day (Pinker 1994). First sentences are short – often described as 'telegraphic speech'. But gradually, inflections are added, along with prepositions, plurals and past tenses, such as 'I wented to nursery'. These '-ed' additions, which are gradually lost, stand out and endorse the claim that children make up their own language structure even when they have not heard such usages before.

As the pre-schoolers gather a huge number of names for things, they go through a time called 'naming explosion' when they point and constantly ask to know what things are called. This precedes the ability to categorise or group objects – the first sign of mathematical learning.

Although language acquisition is not yet fully understood, the fact that children acquire a 'complex and varied use of their language within a few years is nothing short of miraculous' Bee (2002). And when we hear 3-year-olds explaining, cajoling and demanding, we can only agree.

Q **What about the development of mathematical thinking? Sometimes even 3-year-olds will chant numbers up to 10 or even 20.**

At this stage the children are usually simply regurgitating what they have been encouraged to learn by rote. They are enjoying the *sound* of numbers – and this is a good thing – but it doesn't mean they have any real understanding of what they're saying. Children have to *learn* to count objects, giving each a number, and this can be very hard. Their naming skills suddenly disappear and the trail is lost. This is why nurseries start by explaining that they should, for example, choose two items at snack time, or check that three people are at the water tray. They are then seeing the numbers in action. Many number songs are great favourites and they instil the importance of numbers as well.

Some researchers advise that young children should work with small numbers and learn to count forwards 1 to 5 and backwards 5 to 1. If they assign each number to a sequence of blocks or cars, i.e. concrete objects, then they come to understand the basis of addition and subtraction. A good test of understanding is to put out 5 clothes pegs or small toys and ask the child, 'Please give me two'.

Q But maths is more than number work isn't it? What other sorts of activities help children's mathematical development?

Many activities develop mathematical understanding, for example: filling an egg box with small objects is visually reinforcing the number 6, estimating how many apples will fill a basket is an introduction to capacity, while different-sized jugs ready to pour water help an understanding of volume. Recognising shapes such as circles and squares leads to an appreciation of two-dimensional shapes, and later three-dimensional ones; and even colouring-in requires some thinking about directions and stresses, i.e. mathematical concepts. In fact, analysing any of the nursery activities will reveal some mathematical learning. Siphoning water when at the water tray area, and finding how to make the fluid travel quickly and slowly, measuring and weighing at the baking table, giving out one apron to each child at the craft table – all of these are subtle ways of introducing the concept of numbers.

Mathematical language develops as the children experience a range of activities and listen to instructions such as such as 'Pour in *more* water', '*How many* spoons do we need?', 'Make the ball stop *inside the circle*', 'Thread the needle *through* the bead', and so on. Comparisons are also fun and lead to mathematical understanding, e.g. in an activity involving rolling plasticine to strengthen fingers, questions such as 'Who made a long thin snake and who made a short fat one?' will encourage the children to recognise lengths and widths and recognise that the same size ball of plasticine can make different shapes.

Q All of these involve the children in doing things/handling materials. Is this what's meant by concrete learning?

The children need to see and handle objects if they are to understand the effects of manipulating them. Young children live in the present and cannot readily visualise what is not in front of them. Abstract thinking, i.e. envisaging things not present, is a much more sophisticated mode of thinking. The possibilities of mathematical computation increase as this is achieved. But in the nursery, because most children are visual learners, handling, doing and seeing are the most effective learning strategies.

CHANGING CAPACITIES IN THINKING

It is when children are about 3 years old that they begin to use one object as something else, e.g. a yo-yo becomes a toy dog. This is the development of the use of symbols, and can be readily seen when observing children at play.

Q Play moves through developmental phases as the children begin to use symbolism. They become less tied to the here-and-now, and can imagine events that might happen, or, for example, remember going to Grandma's some time ago. What are these stages?

The word 'stages' is not used so much now, due to the realisation that there are rarely abrupt changes – rather one phase develops out of the one before and traces of a former permeate the latter. Also, Piaget's stage theory has been criticised by researchers who found that the adult language he used in his tests might have obscured what the children really knew. When these tests were repeated using child-friendly language the children were found to be able to 'conserve' (to keep a mental image in their heads and not be misled by visual cues), and to understand the perspective of others, at earlier ages than the age of 7 years he had suggested.

There are, however, certain marked progressions that can be observed within children's play. These are listed below.

Sensorimotor play

Very young children, up to about 12 months or so, discover the properties of objects (i.e. their hardness, softness, malleability, their taste and smell), by feeling and tasting, and studying how they move. The high level of sensory input gives this type of play its name. The children also learn to pass objects from hand to hand across the midline of the body, developing their hand dominance and manipulative skills. And, as they reach and grasp, they are learning about distance and direction, i.e. how far the toy is away and how they have to adjust their position to reach it. Letting go is very difficult at this stage, but many important motor skills are being tried out as the children play.

Constructive play

Manipulating one object gradually leads to 2-year-olds experimenting with constructing things, e.g. building blocks, slotting parts of a puzzle together, making something with clay. They handle both large and small objects with increasing dexterity as they develop the pincer grip, turning the pages of books and threading beads. But they mainly identify objects as they really are and use them for their recognised purpose rather than imagining they are something else. Some children have to be taught how to pretend and develop their life skills into pretence, e.g. 'brush your hair, now brush the dolly's hair' is a good way to begin. This is because the children can see these things happening – they are concrete experiences that don't demand too large an imaginative leap.

Pretend play

First phase

Pretend play develops further in the second year, but the children will still use a spoon to feed a doll, or pretend to give a doll a bath, or build bricks in the back of a truck. Although there is a burgeoning element of pretence in that the child may have imagined the doll was dirty or that the blocks were to be used to build a house, the objects are still used for their recognised function and the activities are those that the children have experienced themselves. The children are still tied up in their own perceptions of their world; they still analyse experiences in terms of what has happened to them.

Second phase

Between the ages of 2 and 3 years children begin to use symbols. This is an important development in the use of their imaginations. They discover that *any* object can be used as something else, e.g. a cardboard box can be a bus, with the child loudly ascertaining the imagined object is the real one. By the ages of 3 and 4 years this is the most common type of play.

Third phase: socio-dramatic play

This stage extends imaginative play and social interaction possibilities because children play together to act out a scene. The children depend on their mutual understandings about the roles of the doctor, nurse or bus driver, because these ideas drive the development of the play.

Being involved in shared ploys such as these can allow children to understand a different range of experiences and develop their imaginations too. They may never have been to hospital themselves, but following the lead of another child who has, they will soon don a doctor's coat and confidently apply a bandage or wield a stethoscope. Children learn much from their peer group because the things they copy are usually near their levels of understanding and skill. Adults' suggestions can often be far removed from their own thoughts.

This is the era of the 'imaginary friend'. Imaginary they may be, but they are real to the children who set places at table for them and become distressed if the friend gets 'lost'. Perhaps this is a way to develop empathy and altruism – an imaginary friend is sure to respond to overtures in an acceptable way? Or perhaps a friend who instinctively knows what you mean and doesn't make demands is more comforting than one who voices opinions and expects to share treats? For whatever reason, the imaginary friend is a normal part of childhood and is not a sign of a disturbed or a needy child. This phase will pass when other friendships develop.

Q What resources help develop children's imaginations?

In recent years nurseries have provided more brightly coloured resources than ever before, but to me many of them *dictate* the play rather than letting the children think of ideas for themselves. Children bake at a cooker, supplied with pots and spoons, or they dance with tutus – but they don't seem to fly to the moon on cardboard boxes any more.

Perhaps arranging a group of objects that together don't suggest any *particular* game could stimulate children to imagine something novel, or perhaps children could explain a game, then plan to resource it?

Q Could the developments of all these competences – movement, language and play – be linked in some way?

Certainly, as muscle strength develops, children are enabled to do more things. This applies to both fine and gross motor skills. They need to develop control of the soft palate, lips and tongue before they can articulate words clearly; and once they can do this, they are able to express their intentions and wishes in play situations. Every action requires a level of co-ordination, which comes from muscle control. Table 6.1 is an attempt to link aspects of development in a time-frame. However, some children will travel at unequal speeds and some will have a more uneven pattern of development than others.

▓ TABLE 6.1 Aspects of development

Play	Language	Movement
5 years		
Can initiate or join in complex role-play	Can follow a story without pictures. Can read simple words	Can run and jump, ride a bike and zip a coat. Understands the rules of major games
4 years		
Understands pretence and develops fears of the unknown. Develops imaginative games, not always able to explain 'rules'	Knows colours and numbers. Can explain events, hopes and disappointments	Can climb and swing on large apparatus. Has a developed sense of safety outdoors. Can swim
3 years		
Enjoys group activities, e.g. baking a cake for someone's birthday. Understands turn-taking	Uses complex sentences. Understands directional words and simple comparisons, e.g. big/small; long/short	Can ride a trike; climb stairs with one foot to a step. Climbs in and out of car or bus without help
2½ years		
Develops altruism especially for family members. Understands words such as 'sad', 'happy'	Uses pronouns and past tenses. Adds '-ed' to form own version of past tense	Uses a step-together pattern to climb stairs. Can walk some distance
2 years		
Beginning to play alongside and with a friend for a short time	Rebels. States 'no'. Can form two-word sentences but comprehension far ahead of speech	Still likes to be carried at times but can walk well. Jumping is difficult
18 months		
Sensorimotor play: children explore the properties of objects	Children have a vocabulary of 10 naming-words. Points to make wishes known	Can crawl and walk but can't run or jump. Limbs are strong but balance can be precarious

Q If the children speak early and reach their 'motor' milestones ahead of time, does this mean they are 'intelligent' and will do well all through school?

When results of the first IQ tests for early years children were followed up, they showed little prognostic accuracy. Perhaps they were too limited in the competences they tried to measure or perhaps so many other variables affected the children that the scores were not useful. Today, especially with older children, the scores do seem to allow more accurate assessments, but still need to be regarded with caution, as there can be some variation. For this reason, it is only the extremes of low and high competence that would be measured as routine, because exceptional scores would need additional teaching input.

Q Why should it all be so difficult?

First of all, let's look at the concept of intelligence. With language and physical development, intelligence has a genetic link: temperament can influence attitudes to new learning so this is important as well as scores in IQ tests. But the environment also plays a major part in terms of the opportunities and experiences the children have and how these contribute both to confidence and to general knowledge.

IQ tests really resulted from research that was looking at reasons for the variations in children's capacities to solve problems, to use alternative strategies and to embrace new learning. It sought to measure these differences in order to make prognoses about children's development and appropriate education. The range of IQ scores varies from below 60 (these children need additional support), to 100 (this group would be described as 'average'), to 130–140 or even higher (these children need extended learning opportunities or, if deemed best, acceleration). Within this gifted group there are children who are 'good at everything'. Sometimes called 'garden-variety gifted', they tend to fit in with their peers better than those gifted children who are way beyond the norm in one particular area (these children may find it difficult to interact at the correct level with their peers and they may show more emotional problems).

Of course, the IQ scores can only reflect the competences that were tested, and the realisation that children had a whole range of different strengths has led to different models of intelligence. Arguably the best known is Gardner's (1983) research, which defined six different intelligences: linguistic, musical, logical-mathematical, spatial, bodily kinaesthetic and personal. However, all the different models spelt out the important fact that 'IQ tests failed to measure important qualities that could stand the children in good stead beyond the confines of the school'.

Q What about talented children?

In 2001, several new publications separated 'giftedness' and 'talent'. One, 'A Framework for Gifted and Talented Pupils' (City of Edinburgh Council, 2001) defined giftedness as 'the possession of untrained and spontaneously expressed natural ability, in at least one ability domain to a degree that places the young person in the top 15 per cent of his age peers'. In contrast, they defined talent as achievement in any field of performance. The talented pupils, they explained, were performing at a level significantly beyond what one might expect for their age, but this had come about by sustained rigorous practice built upon interest, enthusiasm and talent.

This document claims that 'quality early years provision has the potential for satisfying gifted and talented youngsters'. However, it also urges practitioners to identify these children, to build relationships with their parents and to build a full profile of competences as a basis for planning further learning.

Q What kinds of activities would suit able children?

Perhaps they could use a digital camera to take outside photographs, then arrange their pictures to illustrate a story they will tell to a small group? Or practitioners could make up a parcel with foreign stamps and use that as a basis for discussion: 'Where has it come from? Who sent it? What could be inside? Who is it for?', and so on. A similar activity could ensue if the children found a toy animal with a notice saying 'Please help me' under a tree in the garden (rather like Paddington Bear). The children could discuss what foods they should provide, where he would sleep, what he was to be called and who would be his friend. Or children could fill a small box of things they have made to sell at a parents' evening. The proceeds would go to children overseas. Such episodes encourage the development of imaginative thinking, and altruism too!

Q And what about children with additional learning needs?

Rather like the gifted and talented differentiation, it is important to identify whether children have a specific learning difficulty, where one aspect of their development is at a much lower level than the others, but where this is unexpected given their other strengths. Such children are likely to need specialised support to compensate for their difficulties, but can do very well in academic work. Children with a global developmental delay find learning across the board problematic and they need help in all aspects of their learning. In 2006 many more children with physical and intellectual difficulties have been moved into mainstream education. However, unless adequate specialised support is provided, they may flounder. Inclusion means very much more than simply being together under the same roof. If the strengths of an inclusive model are to be realised, then resources, in terms of trained personnel and equipment, must match the children's needs. Unfortunately, there are areas where the rhetoric does not yet match the reality.

Thankfully, in the nursery, the higher staff/pupil ratio allows intervention at the correct time and at the most appropriate level; and the play-based curriculum allows all children to cope at their own level. This is very good news.

Chapter 7

Physical and motor development

Q Why is being able to move well in different environments so important? Are children really less healthy and less fit than ever before?

Many young children love to run and jump, swing and climb and they do this with pleasure and with ease. They skip along pavements and hop over the lines that cross their paths. Many continue their active pursuits and enjoy sports training to a high level. In so doing, they are keeping fit and finding a life full of zest. Over more recent years, however, as computer games and safety concerns have intruded, a widespread concern that many of our young children are unfit and overweight has developed. This general change in lifestyle can lead children to avoid the very activities that help to keep them healthy. Both parents being out at work may also result in ready-prepared meals (which usually have a higher salt and fat content) being served more regularly than before. So an increasing number of children are obese; and this in turn has negative effects on their health, their self-esteem and their willingness to be active. Some of the headlines about this trend can be alarming. For example, 'The 10-fold increase in children with diabetes is the tip of the iceberg' (*Telegraph* 28 February 2006, based on a Department of Health report). The article goes on to explain: 'weight-related metabolic syndromes such as high blood pressure, increased cholesterol and fat in the blood are affecting 60,000 children.'

Q Why should this be?

Due to safety concerns, many children are kept indoors rather than 'getting out to play'. This means they are not building a repertoire of movement skills, and this early lack of practice hampers all of their life skills too.

 **FIGURES 7.1–7.3** Some activities where balance, co-ordination and control are essential for success

This is because balance, co-ordination and control of the body are essential if tasks of everyday living are to be efficient. Speaking clearly, zipping a coat, spreading at snack time, using the pincer grip to write and draw, cutting out and colouring in – these are just some of a huge number of movement skills and so it is not difficult to see how poor movement skills affect all aspects of development.

Thankfully, children are now being urged to walk to school, to play out of doors, to play the old-fashioned games such as hopscotch (or 'peevers' as it is known in Scotland). Supermarkets that gave out 'computers for schools' programmes are now distributing tokens for activity clubs. And in many areas where there are few facilities for sport, or little time or money to provide activity clubs, or where children present with difficulties that concern the staff, schools are setting up compensatory movement programmes.

Q Will this counteract the damage that has been done?

The new moves are gratifying, but what is essential is to provide opportunities for all our children to enjoy movement to the extent that they *want* to keep moving, for this stimulates bone density, cardiovascular health and endomorphins. Endomorphins provide that important, feel-good factor that keeps children confident and smiling.

Movement is part of everything we do, from opening our eyes in the morning, to speaking clearly and modulating the tone and pitch of our speech, to carrying out all the activities of daily living and learning. If anyone doubts this, then trying to list activities that do not involve movement can be a salutary experience.

Being able to run and kick a ball, or climb, or ride a bike are the activities children want to do, as well as and, very importantly, at the same time as their friends. If they can't, their friends notice and unfortunately this can lead to teasing. Children who 'can't do' get left out of activities where competence is important and they are not chosen for games. Being part of a group also helps children to be independent. Being judged inadequate because of poor movement does their self-esteem significant damage and may prevent the children trying to improve.

Q Somehow parents don't seem to recognise how important movement is.

That's very true, but when they realise that a good sense of balance helps writing and that the fine motor skills required in music also help mathematics (because a part of each fingertip used in playing an instrument is connected to the maths area in the cerebral cortex), then movement takes its rightful place as the key to learning.

Q How many children find it difficult to move well?

A surprising 6–10 per cent of all children find movement so difficult that all aspects of living and learning are compromised (Dyspraxia Foundation 2001). Boys appear on this list much more than girls, in a ratio of 4:1 or 5:1.

Q So, what can practitioners do to support children who have problems?

It is vital to find out the real cause. It may be inability to do the movement itself, and this could be due to a neurological cause (e.g. poor myelination, see Figure 7.4), which impacts on balance, co-ordination and control, or it may be the planning and organising (the mental preparation that precedes an action) that hinders the outcome.

So practitioners must:

- observe carefully, so that they can record what is amiss;
- understand why the children are experiencing these difficulties, based on evidence gleaned from observations;
- design movement programmes which will help the children's development and help them to practise regularly every single day.

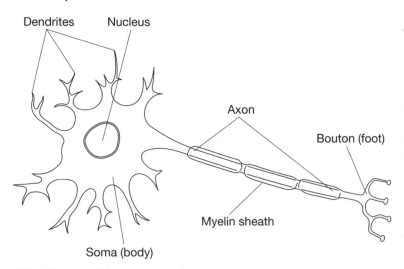

FIGURE 7.4 The structure of a neuron

MOVEMENT ACTIVITIES, WITH OBSERVATION/ TEACHING POINTS

Q What skills need to be developed?

Activities to develop body and spatial awareness, balance, co-ordination and control should be part of everyday practice for they are essential prerequisites in every fine motor, gross motor and manipulative skill. A small sample can be seen in Table 7.1.

TABLE 7.1 Some fine, gross and manipulative motor skills

Fine motor (using the small muscle groups)	Gross motor (using the large muscle groups)	Everyday manipulative skills (using both muscle groups)
Fastening buttons/tying laces	Crawling, walking, running and jumping, hopping, turning corners, i.e. all the basic movement patterns	Cleaning teeth; wiping at the toilet. Writing, painting, drawing, threading, spreading at snack, picking things up and letting go
Articulating words. Using gestures to communicate meaning	Crawling though a tunnel	Opening the door. Packing a bag/lunch box. Organising equipment
Picking up objects using the pincer (tripod) grip	Throwing and catching/ kicking a ball	Tidying up. Manipulating a mouse/keyboard. Texting etc.
Letting objects go	Climbing stairs	Eating at mealtimes. Using a knife and fork
Stirring, pouring, mixing	Hopping	Fastening up a jacket
Writing and drawing	Skipping	Jumping onto a bus
Doing a jigsaw; using Lego	Building bricks	Riding a bike

Q This is a much wider view of movement than we had thought initially. We were thinking about activities like climbing on the frame or rolling on the mats. Maybe it would be a good idea to make a list of movements that are especially important in our own setting? We could use that as a focus for observation. But how would we record improvement?

You could use the symbols 0 (meaning can't do), 1 (OK) and 2 (very proficient) to record competence, and then recheck progress every two weeks or so to see whether improvement has been made. This is why it is very important to include the date when recording observations. The important thing is to keep the records very simple for children who *can* cope, but to record exact details for those who find movement difficult. It's also important to try to *extend* the able children, perhaps by asking them to explain what they plan to do. For this they need some movement language, e.g. 'I'm going "under" the skittle and "through" the hoop to stand "opposite" the tree'. So movement helps maths too! Also remember you can't see every child every day. Make a careful list so that you include them all over a weekly or fortnightly slot.

But, of course, being able to do all these things doesn't happen overnight and there is a developmental sequence that differentiates 'performance' over the age range, e.g. while 3-year-olds might still use the step-together pattern in climbing stairs, 4-year-olds should be able to use the one-foot-at-a-time action, provided they have stairs at home.

Q When should practitioners begin to assess children's movement skills?

1   In a general way: this should be as soon as possible, to note things the children find straightforward and actions they find difficult.
2   More specifically: once the children are at ease in their surroundings; when they are familiar with any apparatus, and have built relationships with their practitioners. Then close observation can reveal perceptual or sensory difficulties as well as the more obvious movement ones.

Of course, children have different experiences before coming to nursery/school as well as different temperaments, and these will influence the way they approach new activities. This means that assessments should

TABLE 7.2 An observational record of basic movement patterns

Crawling	Standing/sitting still	Running and jumping
16 April 2007	18 April 2007	22 April 2007
Rowan (2yrs 6 mths)		
0 – still unable to balance on all fours; suspect lack of arm strength – test hand grip, shoulder stability	1 – improving but needs time to focus	
Charlene (3 yrs 4 mths)		
2	2	1 – still rushes take-off – lacks sense of where her feet are – do foot awareness jingles
Martin (4 yrs 6 mths)		
2	2 – but can't wait	2 – now ask him what he needs to do to jump higher
Jilly (5 yrs 6 mths)		
1 – prefers to pull along on her front	2 – but appears solidly fixed to the spot. She collapses into herself – aim to develop tummy and back strength (spinning cone)	0 – can't cope with the co-ordination demands – practise jumping on her own

not happen once but be repeated over a period of time. They can then contribute towards a profile of achievement for passing on to 'big school' or be used as evidence to speed access to expert help. If additional learning needs are suspected, it is helpful to video the children (parental permission will be needed), because visuals are often clearer than written descriptions. Video also allows recordings to be reviewed and shared so that more/less experienced eyes can give practitioners confidence in making decisions about intervention.

Q Are there other things that should be checked out first?

Before starting to assess, it can be revealing to consider whether other factors, even inflexible shoes, may prevent the children moving well.

If this is not done, then interventions to support the children may be based on incorrect information. The list shown in Figure 7.5 offers some guidance.

Q OK, but what are the questions that we should ask about movement itself?

A first checklist is suggested in Figure 7.6.

When staff suspect a problem, then arranging the big apparatus to highlight the difficulty can provide evidence of whether it is or is not there. When one boy was thought to have poor arm strength, the staff put out a long tunnel so that he had to crawl through, then pull out at the end. What happened was that the child used his head as a lever to pull himself through. He had developed a strategy to compensate, but hiding the problem was not going to make it go away.

These preliminary baseline assessments are very useful. Often parents may (mistakenly) not be too concerned about poor movement competence until the child finds writing impossible. The difficulties will have been there in the child – they don't suddenly appear – but in the early years, parents tend to fasten coats, tie laces and carry bags just to save time and so the children's difficulties aren't immediately apparent.

Q So how does movement hamper writing?

Writing is a movement skill. The child should sit in a balanced position with feet steady on the floor and with a desk at elbow height. An inclined writing board can prevent unnecessary and confusing movements of the head, and a thick pencil with a special grip (there are many on the market to suit all hands) can support the tripod or pincer grip. It is also important that the sitting position of right- and left-handed children is considered to save elbows clashing and possibly tempers fraying. Right-handed children should be on the right.

Sometimes, if writing letters back to front persists, it can indicate a lack of hand dominance, i.e. not knowing which hand to use, which should be in place by age 3 years. Practitioners can help children to decide and then remind them to use their more proficient side when they try other activities.

In a game of tossing a beanbag into a waste-paper bin, Grethe was asked: 'Which hand scored the most goals?' Once she was sure, she was gently reminded of her choice at painting, threading and spreading.

Does the child have	Yes	No	Comment/severity/medication/ other aids required
Sensory difficulties, e.g.			
1 Poor balance?			
2 Poor hearing?			
3 Restricted vision?			
4 Allergies?			
5 Asthma?			
Communication difficulties, e.g.			
1 Understanding?			
2 Articulating?			
3 Explaining?			
Personality/behaviour difficulties, e.g.			
1 Shyness?			
2 Aggression?			
3 Withdrawn			
4 Slow to warm up?			
5 Low self-esteem?			

FIGURE 7.5 Differentiating between fine, gross and manipulative skills

Can the child	Yes	No	Comment: e.g. is clumsy, falls over easily
Move with control? i.e. judge the correct amount of strength and speed that is required?			
Crawl, using the cross-lateral pattern?			
Cope with steps-up and -down?			
Judge drops safely? Leave the ground (jump, hop or skip)?			
Consistently use the same hand/ foot?			
Work confidently at/cross the midline of the body?			
Change direction easily?			
Look in control of their own body?			

 FIGURE 7.6 A checklist of important indicators of motor development

And so there are simple strategies to solve specific difficulties, but when these persist, a daily movement programme is the best way forward.

Q When can I do a programme? Does it need to be in one block each day?

Not necessarily. When you want to use large apparatus then it is best to have a *planned* time, so that someone has responsibility for checking all the safety points in advance of the children arriving.

Q How do you bring out the intellectual component with very young children?

You might ask the most able children to help with the organisation and resourcing, setting tasks such as:

- Can you sort the coloured bands into bundles of the same colour for me?
- Can you sort this bundle out so that I have the same number of red, blue and green bands?
- What apparatus should we choose for balancing today?
- Can you make up the rules for a game that uses a big ball, but has benches for goals instead of a net? Think of how the game starts, how a goal is scored and what you need to do to ensure the game stays safe for all the players.

Movement activities can be interspersed with sedentary work, even within the confines of a classroom. If there is restricted space, allowing one table of children to march in and out the spaces without touching can give respite and help concentration.

Q Can you help us with more ideas for activities?

The following ideas cover gross movements, fine motor skills and manipulative skills. I'm sure that, once you start, ideas will come flooding in (see Bibliography for books of ideas). It's important to remember that even very simple movements (e.g. walking along a bench) should be done well, before complications (e.g. carrying a hoop, or stepping over beanbags) are introduced.

ACTIVITIES TO HELP PROMOTE BODY AND SPATIAL AWARENESS, BALANCE, CO-ORDINATION AND CONTROL

Note: The aim of any programme is to have children improve their basic movement patterns and to be able to adapt these in different environments, e.g. a child can progress from learning to crawl on the floor to crawling along a bench, then an inclined bench, and then crawling up stairs, for the crawling and the climbing pattern are one and the same. The changed environment adds variety and challenge. If children 'cannot do', then simplifying the resources (e.g. catching a balloon that travels more slowly than a ball), or modifying the environment (e.g. having the child kick a ball into an empty goal rather than having to outwit a goalie) can give a positive start.

KEY FACTORS IN DEVELOPING EFFICIENT MOVEMENT

Body awareness – children have to be able to feel where their body parts are

Simon says and similar games

(See Table 7.3 for an example of 'Simon says'.) These games are always well liked and they are excellent for helping children with poor body awareness recognise and feel where their different body parts are. These activities develop the children's sense of body boundary too. This means that they recognise where their bodies end and the outside world begins, an important skill which contributes to deft movement and safety, e.g. placing a cup firmly on a table (rather than precariously on the edge), or recognising where to stop at the kerb.

Many nursery jingles are based on promoting body awareness, e.g. 'Heads, shoulders, knees and toes', 'Under the spreading chestnut tree', 'Tap time' (in Macintyre, 2003).

Stressing movement during everyday activities in the nursery

As the children are engaged in their nursery activities, comments such as 'Hold your arm into your side and you'll be strong enough to pour

TABLE 7.3 'Simon says'

Simon says (copying and then without copying)	Look for	Help
Put two hands on your head	Slow reaction; two arms moving at different speeds	Use body parts the children can see, e.g. knees, toes
Stretch two arms into the sky. Look up to see your fingers (stars twinkling suggests movement)	Children overbalancing, especially when head position changes and fingers move. Bent arms – one or both	1 Stand against wall to help balance 2 Face wall and climb fingers up (Incy wincy spider)
Sit down and stretch your legs out in front. Lean back on your hands. Move feet towards and away together then alternately	Slumping trunks, heads poking forward. Head nodding as feet move. Inability to do the alternate foot action	Count out, 'Hello toes, Goodbye toes' to help children recognise the rhythm of the action. Remind them to 'sit tall with long straight backs'
Crossing the midline		
Put one hand on the other knee. Use twirling ribbons to make figures of eight across the body	Children who can't cross the midline	Give the children a beanbag in each hand. Try 'semaphore' type actions where one hand stays still but the other moves to meet it

the water into the jug without spilling' or 'Look how close together your hands are when you are threading/spreading' can help develop body awareness.

Q How do we make children aware of their backs?

Ideally, use a spinning cone. To make the cone turn, the children must begin the action by leaning back and pushing, then the abdominal muscles must work hard till the back takes over again.

Table 7.4 shows some other ideas.

TABLE 7.4 Some other ideas for movement activities

Activity: *Angels in the snow*	Look for	Help
Lie on the floor – open and close legs feeling the backs of the legs on the floor	Children who cannot move their legs together without looking to see what is happening.	Do the action sitting first so that they can see the movement and internalise the feel of it
Sweep the arms overhead (backs of arms on the floor)	Bent arms – suggest they turn palms up – this pulls the shoulders back	If the arm sweep is difficult, allow the children to hold a beanbag in each hand
Do both actions together	Can they join two hands together above their heads and bump two feet together when they meet at the midline of the body?	Give plenty time. Check shoulder rigidity. DO NOT FORCE any action – ask for physio-therapy if child cannot relax the shoulders
Children lie in a line or in a circle. As they sweep hands up they should touch their neighbour's hand. Feet can touch as the legs sweep apart	Check timing and awareness of movement to the side. Can the children time the action without looking?	Check backs don't lift from the floor – if so the stretch is too wide – narrow the activity

Q If children appear floppy, how can we make them stronger? Or if they are stiff, what then?

(Table 7.5 shows some ideas.) Some resistance is needed to make the muscles work harder while helping the child's mobility needs limbs to move through a greater range, e.g. use twirling ribbons to encourage the children to stretch through the full range of movement. Pulling through water in the swimming pool or even in the water tray, creating roads in wet sand and moulding wet clay are all useful ideas. If the children are unhappy with the texture of clay, they can often tolerate 'Theraputty'. Theraputty is a clean malleable substance (which children who dislike 'dirty clay' are usually happy to use). There are five strengths, so the density of the material can be changed as strength develops. The children can pull it, mould it and stretch it. One enjoyable task is to find hidden

TABLE 7.5 Some other ideas for strengthening activities

Activity	Look for	Help
Popping bubble paper	Fingers without sufficient strength	Pull fingers through water; build castles in the sand – give lots of strengthening work
Winding a yo-yo	Children who cannot work with two hands doing different things at the midline of the body	Use large jigsaws or puzzles where the action happens at or crosses the midline. Woodwork is popular
Threading beads	Children who close one eye – check whether this happens at other times – check with optician	Begin in a sitting position to minimise balance demands. This is an aiming practice – check pincer/tripod grip
Nursery darts	Check stance for the start of an overarm throw (opposite foot forward)	Transfer of weight from back to front foot. Call out rhythm 1,2, . . . 3; 3 is throw
Quickly transferring balls, shuttlecocks, reels, etc. (small objects of different sizes and shapes) from one pail to another (time challenge)	Difficulty in grasping and letting go	Increase the space between the pails. This means the required hand actions are slower and less demanding
Batting a shuttlecock with a small wooden bat	Children who can't time the contact – begin with very small hits	Support the hand to keep the face of the bat flat. The sound should help the rhythm
Playing an old piano	This allows children to concentrate on their hands. They enjoy the feedback	Check whether some fingers in particular lack strength

FIGURE 7.7
Making handprints
helps develop hand
awareness and
finger strength

treasure inside a ball of Theraputty. This involves the children in lots of
pulling, which strengthens fingers, forearms and even shoulders.

Gross motor skills

Crawling (to help co-ordination, balance and spatial orientation)

(See Table 7.6 for some crawling activities.) Teach the crawling action
using a jingle, e.g.

> Right hand, left knee on we go
> Left hand right knee, who can show?
> Crawling forwards 1, 2, 3
> You can do it easily!

TABLE 7.6 Some crawling activities

Activity	Look for	Help
First of all, ask the children to take up the crawling (table) position. This is a safe position where balance is not difficult. The children feel secure	Children who can't keep a flat back. Wobbly limbs – arms or legs – children who sit back or topple to the side	Place a beanbag on the small of the back – ask the children to keep it steady there. Emphasise strong arms and legs
Move the body from side to side or forwards/ backwards if they can keep the beanbag in position – then they can try to toss the beanbag off by straightening their legs. They should always come back to the crawling (table) position	Children who can't regain the table position after moving – they may have to sit back or their arms may collapse	Strengthening work for arms and legs. Check if children can't move weight forward onto arms (which should stay straight and strong)
In the table position again, the children can pick up beanbags from the floor and toss them into a bin	This means one arm moves and the weight adjusts to balance on three limbs. This helps them (a) to learn to keep balanced when one limb moves; and (b) gives them some idea about direction and distance	They can score a point when the beanbag goes in! For progressions, ask the children to move further back from the bin Circles drawn round the bin can give scoring targets

When 'Kicking horses' (an activity like a handstand with one knee remaining on the ground and the other leg swung upwards) is used,

Make your arms and hands so strong,
Stretch one leg out, make it long
Swing it up now, really high,
Look – it nearly hits the sky!

Note: Using jingles helps to develop the children's sense of rhythm, which is important in all movement, as well as in speaking, writing and reading. It also helps mathematical skills, e.g. learning times tables.

TABLE 7.7 More activities (1)

Activity	Note	Help
Rolling sideways from the crawling position	This is a safety practice that should first happen on mats. From the crawling or table position the children should tuck one arm through the other, follow it with their head and roll over onto their shoulder and back, sustaining enough momentum to roll right round to kneeling. The children should understand that they are taking their weight on the rounded padded bits and that elbows, the points of shoulders and knees need to be protected	Safety in landing. The children need to realise that this skill, i.e. learning to meet the ground safely, will protect them should they fall. They must not fall on outstretched arms else jarring or even clavicle breakage may occur
Pencil rolls	Can the children stretch out while keeping their arms rounded into their bodies?	Ask, 'Can you push your toes long?', 'Do you feel where they are?'

LISTS OF ACTIVITIES TO DEVELOP FINE MOTOR SKILLS

Finger awareness: finger, hand, arm and shoulder strengthening

1   It is essential that children develop dexterity, i.e. being able to handle small objects with control. This comes through practice in manipulating objects that provide some resistance (strengthening work) and learning to use the pincer grip.

TABLE 7.8 More activities (2)

Activity	Check	Help
Walking	Poise, balance and control. The shoulders should be relaxed and low with the arms swinging naturally	Count out a rhythm if the stride pattern is unequal
Stepping over bands on the floor	Check the smooth transfer of weight	
Walking in straight lines, forwards and backwards, then along curves and then with abrupt changes of direction	Note the children who can't change direction. If their toes are pointing in, the whole position of the leg will hinder the change	Make children aware of placing their foot – look at footprints in the sand. Emphasise toes forward. If this 'hen-toed' action persists, seek physio-therapy help
Walking through the space made by two facing benches. The activity begins with the benches far apart and gradually being moved together	The aim is for the children to be aware of objects at their side and to judge the width of their body/movement pattern in relation to the available space. (This develops spatial awareness and laterality or sidedness)	Children who are tentative because they cannot see if they will be able to get through the space. Add other 'getting through' activities, e.g. passing a hoop over their head to the floor. This lets them judge the space around them

To do this, children need to become aware of how they are using their fingers, hands and arms. They also have to be helped to develop hand dominance.

2 It is vital that children learn to use two hands at the midline of the body – preferably doing different things, e.g. opening a jar, unscrewing nuts on a bolt, or threading beads. This is bilateral integration. They also have to be able to cross the midline. Figure-of-eight actions, e.g. drawing in the air – perhaps of the first letter of their name – helps this.

3 Reflecting on existing activities in the light of promoting strength and dexterity often shows that some minor organisational change means that they can provide a greater

121

pay-off, e.g. at baking time, let those with poor hand strength be the first to mix the butter and sugar for there is more resistance when the butter is hard.

4   Rolling out dough, using scone cutters (gingerbread men) and placing the dough on baking trays – then eating the results – gives a satisfying sequence of events. Stressing the order helps planning and organising.

5   Mashing potatoes with a potato masher can strengthen the shoulders, arms and hands. The children can then mould the mashed potatoes into balls (adding cheese that they have grated) to make croquettes, roll the croquettes in egg and breadcrumbs and pop them in the oven to make a tasty snack.

Dramatic ideas to show a change of quality in walking

Build small group (dramatic) activities based on walking. In these the quality of the walk should change. For example:

1   On a cold frosty morning walk briskly to school.

- Blow out to make 'frosty breath'. Blow on cupped hands. Shake tingling fingers (these actions can challenge balance).
- Swoop arms round to keep warm (hand and back awareness).
- See a friend and wave. Run over to join hands and jump up and down together to keep warm.

2   It is very hot in the forest. You are trying to spot butterflies and humming birds. You mustn't make a sound.

- Prowl quietly through the undergrowth (slow careful walking at a low level).
- Use big sweeping actions to clear a path (balance challenge).
- Curl up quietly and listen to the humming sounds (awareness of rounded backs).
- Notice a snake slithering through the undergrowth.
- Jump up and rush away – leap up into your tree house.

This can be built up into a dramatic dance if different children take different parts, e.g. humming birds, butterflies, snakes, leopards, etc. The children can describe a series of events, and the teacher can add descriptive words linking a class theme and supporting literacy development.

Many more ideas are in *Jingle Time* (see Macintyre, 2003).

As children learn to move, they learn about how to control their bodies and keep them safe. They learn how to run and skip with others and how to catch and kick a ball. These skills allow them to take part in activities with others so their social development benefits. And, as they grow and make judgements about how to care for themselves, there are intellectual and moral elements (e.g. if I keep fit and learn about nutrition, I won't need hospital resources) in this too. So, while each aspect of development is worthy of separate study, analysis is best seen in the context of synthesis, for children use them all together all of the time.

Bibliography

Ainsworth, M. (1972) 'Attachment and dependency: A comparison' in J.L. Gerwirtz (ed.) *Attachment and Dependency*. Washington, DC: VH Winston

Bee, H. (2002) *The Developing Child*. New York: HarperCollins College Publishers

Bee, H. (2004) *The Growing Child*. New York: HarperCollins College Publishers

Bellhouse, B., Johnson, J. and Fuller, F. (2005) *Empathy: Promoting Resilience and Emotional Intelligence for Young People Aged 7–11*. London: Lucky Duck Publishing/Paul Chapman

Bowlby, J. (1988) *A Secure Base: Clinical Applications of Attachment Theory*. London: Routledge

City of Edinburgh Council (2001) *A Framework for Gifted and Talented Pupils*. Edinburgh: City of Edinburgh Council

Cohen, D. (1990) *The Development of Play*. New York: New York University Press

Collins, M. (2005) *It's OK to be Sad. Activities to Help Children Manage Loss, Grief and Bereavement*. London: Lucky Duck Publishing/Paul Chapman

Davies, G. and Cummings, E.M. (1994) 'Marital conflict and child adjustment'. *Psychological Bulletin*, 116, 387–411

Dowling, M. (2004) *Young Children's Personal, Social and Emotional Development*. London: Paul Chapman

Dyspraxia Foundation (2001) *Report: Praxis Makes Perfect*. Hitchin: Dyspraxia Foundation

Eisenberg, N. (1990) *The Development of Prosocial Behaviour*. Hillsdale, NY: Erlbaum

Eisenberg, N. (1992) *The Caring Child*. Cambridge, MA: Harvard University Press

Gardner, H. (1983) *Frames of Mind: The Theory of Multiple Intelligences*. New York: Basic Books

Isaacs, S. (1933) *Social Development in Young Children*. London: Routledge

Katz, L.F. and Gottman, J.M. (1993) 'Patterns of marital conflict predict children's internalising and externalising behaviours'. *Developmental Psychology*, 29, 940–50

Kohlberg, L. (1969) 'Stages and sequence: The cognitive–developmental approach to socialisation' in D.A. Goslin (ed.) *Handbook of Socialisation Theory and Research*. Chicago, IL: Rand McNally

Maccoby, E. and Martin, E. (1990) 'Socialisation in the context of the family' in E.M. Hetherington (ed.) *Handbook of Child Psychology Vol. 4*. New York: Wiley

Macintyre, C. (2003) *Jingle Time*. London: David Fulton Publishers

Macintyre, C. (2005) *Identifying and Supporting Children with Additional Learning Needs: Listen to the Children*. London: Routledge

Macintyre, C. and McVitty, K. (2003) *Planning the Pre-5 Setting*. London: David Fulton Publishers

Macintyre, C. and McVitty, K. (2004) *Movement and Learning in the Early Years*. London: Sage/Paul Chapman Publications

Melhuish, E.C. (1990) *Research on Day Care for Young Children in the United Kingdom: International Perspectives*. London: Routledge

Moore, C. (2004) *George and Sam*. New York: Viking Press

Murray, M. and Keene, C. (1998) *The ABC of Bullying*. Dublin: Mercier Press

Myers, B.J. (1999) 'Mother–infant bonding. The status of this critical period hypothesis'. *Developmental Review*, 4, 240–278

Peer, L. (2004) 'Otitis media: A new hypothesis in dyslexia'. Paper presented at the BDA International Conference, University of Warwick, March 2004

Piaget, J. (1932) *The Moral Judgement of the Child*. Harmondsworth: Penguin

Pinker, S. (1994) *The Language Instinct: How the Mind Creates Language*. New York: William Morow

Schaffer, H.R. (1990) *Social Development*. Oxford: Blackwell Publishing

Scottish Executive (Learning and Teaching Scotland 2005) *Birth to Three: Supporting our Youngest Children*. Edinburgh: Scottish Executive

Smith, P.K., Blades, M. and Cowie, H. (2002) *Understanding Children's Development* (3rd edition) Oxford: Blackwell Publishers

Thomas, A. and Chess, S. (1977) *Temperament and Development*. New York: Bruner/Mazel

Trevarthen, C. (1974) 'Play for Tomorrow'. Video presentation, Edinburgh University

Winston, R. (2006) *Child of Our Time*. Television series for BBC1

Index

Relevant Figures and Tables are indicated in *italic* type. **Bold** type indicates complete chapters.

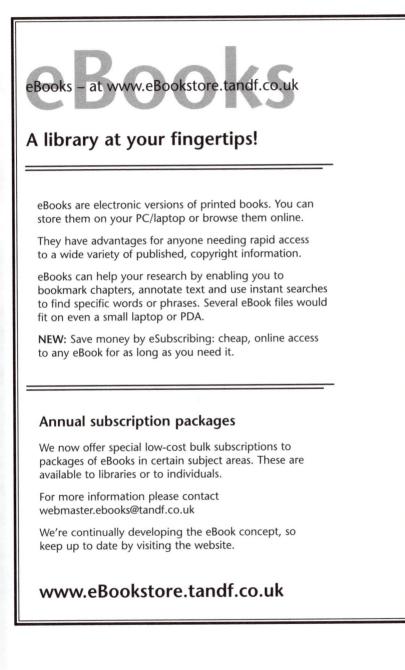